THE BAZAR BOOK

OF

DECORUM.

THE CARE OF THE PERSON,
MANNERS,
ETIQUETTE,
and
CEREMONIALS.

"Those thousand decencies that daily flow
From all her words and actions."
MILTON.

NEW YORK:
HARPER & BROTHERS, PUBLISHERS,
FRANKLIN SQUARE.
1873.

PREFACE.

This book is an attempt to raise the subject of which it treats to its proper connection with health, morals, and good taste.

The title is due to the fact that the author has embodied in the text several articles which were originally published by him in *Harper's Bazar*. These, though they form but a small portion of the whole work, may be recognized by some of the many readers of that popular periodical; if so, it is hoped that they will be thought of sufficient value to justify their reproduction in the present form.

CONTENTS.

CHAPTER V.

CHAPTER VI.

CHAPTER VII.

CHAPTER VIII.

THE

BAZAR BOOK OF DECORUM.

CHAPTER I.

Ceremonial Observances founded on Common Sense.—The peculiar Necessity for Americans to cultivate Politeness.—Advantage of Politeness.—Duke of Marlborough.

It is quite a mistake to suppose that the ceremonial observances of society are merely a set of edicts arbitrarily established by the capricious tyrant, Fashion, for the government only of her slavish subjects. Polite conduct is not necessarily more exclusive than correct speaking. The laws of the one are indeed, like those of the other, founded upon the usage of the refined few, but there is no better reason why these should enjoy a monopoly of good manners than of good grammar. There are many, however, who seem to think that social ceremonies are so many frivolous affectations by which the wealthy or fashionable strive to raise themselves to a factitious elevation above others, and consequently refuse all observance of them with scorn. It is an unfortunate thing for general culture when the many acquire such a prejudice against the few that in their aversion to their pretentious superiority they reject their real excellence. The small class of the rich and refined have time to cultivate the elegancies of life; and although, in the excess of their leisure, they superadd a variety of frivolous ceremonies, their example in what is practically useful should be followed. Wesley used to say, when advocating the adaptation of the music of the opera and theatre to the sacred songs of the Church, that he did not know why the devil should have all the best tunes. We may ask, with equal reason, why Fashion should have all the good manners.

It would be easy to show that many ceremonious observances which appear at first sight frivolous are founded upon a solid basis of common sense. Consider, for example, that rule of the dinner-table, Do not ask twice for soup. This appears at first sight both silly and arbitrary. It is, however, a very sensible ordinance, and is to be justified by the laws of health, and the general comfort and convenience. The soup, being a fluid substance, can easily be absorbed in small quantities, and, thus taken, is a good preparative for the solidities of the dinner. If, however, the stomach is deluged with it, the appetite and digestion become weakened, and there is neither the inclination to eat nor the power to digest the more substantial food essential to the due nutrition of the body. As for the convenience or comfort of the single-plate rule, no one can deny it who has ever looked upon an array of hungry guests whose eager appetite for the coming roast has been forced to an impatient delay by some social monster capable of asking twice for soup. The cook in the mean time is, of course, thrown out in his calculations, and the dish, when it does come at last, is either spoiled by overcooking, or cold from being withdrawn so long from the fire. The guests thus are not only tried in temper by a protracted expectation, but balked of their anticipated enjoyment.

The advantage of not putting the knife in the mouth will be obvious, we suppose, to all who are conscious that the one can cut and the other is capable of being cut. There is an excellent chemical reason for that other table rule which forbids the use of a knife of steel with the fish, the ordinary sauces of which combine with the metal, and produce a composition neither wholesome nor appetizing.

All that is worth borrowing from the fashionable code can be had without much additional cost either of time or money. For example, a table can be well set as expeditiously and with no more expense than if every article upon it was placed out of line with its fellows. There is no economy, pecuniary or otherwise, in serving a dish to the right instead of the left of the guest, while the latter has the advantage not only of being the correct thing, but the most convenient. So, too, there can be no minutes saved from the dinner-hour by gorging the stomach with pie or pudding in advance of the beef and cabbage, while there is the very serious waste of appetite upon the less nutritious food.

The great purpose of the rules of etiquette is to inculcate good manners, and thus render us mutually agreeable. It is, therefore, especially incumbent upon all Americans to know and obey them, for it is impossible for us to avoid contact. We are all forced, in spite of individual objections and protests, to put into practice the national theory of equality. We must mix together, and it therefore behooves us, for our own comfort, to make the mixture as smooth and uniform as possible.

In no country in the world are general good manners so indispensable as in this democratic country. In Europe, where, in society as at the railway stations, different classes are recognized and kept apart by insurmountable barriers and vigilant guards, it is possible, if you happen to be among the high-bred "firsts" or decent "seconds," to endure the existence of the unruly "thirds." These last, in fact, when viewed at a convenient remoteness of distance, are not without their interest. Their unkempt hair, botched and greasy suits, rude manners, and coarse vernacular, are parts of the European picture, and by their own homely raciness, as well as the contrast they afford to the brilliancy of their superiors, seem essential to its effect. To look at a rough and unwashed from the safe distance of European social distinction, by which he is toned down to the picturesqueness of one of Murillo's lousy beggar-boys, is one thing; it is quite another, however, to have him at your elbow on railway and at hotel, where you can hear, feel, and smell him. It is obvious, therefore, that the rough and dirty are quite out of place in this country, where, if they exist, they are sure to be close at your side. Universal cleanliness and good manners are essential to a democracy. This must be generally recognized and acted upon, or the refined will seek in other countries the exclusiveness which will secure for them that nicety of life essential to its enjoyment, and we shall be left alone to wallow in our own brutality and foulness.

There is no reason why propriety of manners should not be as general in the United States as it is exclusive in most countries. With our facility of mixture, any leaven we have can be easily made to pervade the whole mass. There is no vested right, in this country at least, in decency and cleanliness. We can all be, if we please, what we are so fond of calling ourselves, gentlemen and ladies.

There is, however, an idea somewhat prevalent, especially among our newly-arrived Democrats, that it is an essential principle of democracy to be rude and dirty. They forget that they are no longer, in this country, as they might have been in their own, in an antagonistic position to every cleanly and polite person. A man who has his shoes blacked and takes his hat off to a lady is not in the United States necessarily an aristocrat. It is this erroneous notion, which we venture to say is an imported one, that decency of person and manners must be associated with aristocracy, which keeps us still supplied with so many of the rough and dirty sort. Not a few of our public men are responsible for the encouragement of this vulgar faith in democratic foulness. They affect a carelessness of dress and coarseness of talk and manners with the idea that they thus assimilate and make themselves more acceptable to the multitude. We doubt, however, the success of an expedient which is any thing but a compliment to even the rudest and dirtiest. We were once a witness to a signal failure of a political orator who ventured to try this kind of tactics upon a New England audience. "I have not come," he said, "to be received with any ceremonious attention, but to *take a drink and a chaw* of tobacco* with you." This might have gone down in Slum Hall of his native city, where he was wont to stir the "fierce democracy," but his audience of Puritan decency and sobriety would have been less shocked by the dash of a genuine bucket of cold water than by this vulgar suggestion of the groggery.

Philosophers and men of the world are alike of the opinion that propriety of manners is to be commended, not only for its own sake, but for the social advantage it gives. Locke, in his celebrated treatise, makes good breeding, by which he means refined behavior, an essential element of the character of the well educated. Lord Chesterfield rates so highly the graces, as he terms them, that he seems to give them a value beyond that of the virtues. It appears

* Provincialism for "quid" or "cud."

that his lordship would have much preferred his son, whom he strove so hard, but vainly, to endow with all the graces, to be an elegant rogue than an honest lout. He evidently thought that refinement of manners did more to gain the whole world, and was therefore more desirable, for he took little account of the possibility of the loss of a soul, than obedience to the twelve commandments. He certainly gives a remarkable example of its power. "Of all the men that ever I knew in my life (and I knew him extremely well), the late Duke of Marlborough," says he, "preserved the graces in the highest degree, not to say engrossed them; and, indeed, he got the most by them, for I will venture (contrary to the custom of profound historians, who always assign deep causes for great events) to ascribe the better half of the Duke of Marlborough's greatness and richness to those graces. He was eminently illiterate; wrote bad English, and spelled it still worse. He had no share of what is commonly called *parts;* that is, he had no brightness, nothing shining in his genius. He had, most undoubtedly, an excellent good plain understanding, with sound judgment; but these alone would probably have raised him but something higher than they found him, which was page to King James the Second's queen. There the graces protected and promoted him; for, while he was an ensign of the Guards, the Duchess of Cleveland, then favorite mistress to King Charles the Second, struck by those very graces, gave him five thousand pounds, with which he immediately bought an annuity for his life, of five hundred pounds a year, of my grandfather, Halifax, which was the foundation of his subsequent fortune. His figure was beautiful, but his manner was irresistible by either man or woman. It was by this engaging, graceful manner that he was enabled, during all his war, to connect the various and jarring powers of the Grand Alliance, and to carry them on to the main object of the war, notwithstanding their private and separate views, jealousies, and wrongheadednesses. Whatever court he went to (and he was often obliged to go himself to some testy and refractory ones), he as constantly prevailed and brought them into his measures. The Pensionary Heinsius, a venerable old minister, grown gray in business, and who had governed the Republic of the United Provinces for more than forty years, was absolutely governed by the Duke of Marlborough, as that republic feels to this day. He was always cool, and nobody ever observed the least variation in his countenance. He could refuse more gracefully than other people could grant, and those who went away from him the most dissatisfied as to the substance of their business, were yet charmed with him, and in some degree comforted by his manner. With all his gentleness and gracefulness, no man living was more conscious of his situation, nor maintained his dignity better."

It was hardly necessary, however, to evoke from the shades of history so grave an exemplar of the graces as the great victor of Blenheim to inculcate the necessity in these days of attention to the refined civilities of life. These have become so general, and so essential to the conduct of society, that no shop-boy or kitchen-maid is either entirely ignorant of, or ventures wholly to disregard them.

CHAPTER II.

The Obligation to cultivate Beauty.—Notions of Beauty.—Beauty and Health.—American Looks.—Their good and bad Qualities.—How to improve the Bad and preserve the Good.—The Skin.

THOUGH we may not give full assent to Madame de Pompadour's dictum that the chief duty of woman is to be beautiful, we do not hesitate to confess the opinion that it is a social obligation not only of her sex, but that of the male, to make the best possible appearance. A code such as that of good manners, which recognizes as its main purpose to render us mutually agreeable, can hardly be complete if it does not contain rules for the proper management of the person. It would seem to be an essential part of politeness to commend ourselves to each other by such a care of our bodies that they may not only be free from offense, but a source of positive pleasure to those with whom we are in communion. We ought not to be content merely with having our bodily presence endured, but should, as far as it lies in our power, make ourselves physically attractive. We so far agree, then, with Madame de Pompadour as to acknowledge that it is the duty of woman, and also of man, to be beautiful if they can.

It is a curious fact that few women are competent judges of what is essentially a quality of their own—female beauty. It is not easy for any one to define it, though we all recognize its presence. It depends so much upon expression and action, which are essentially mobile, that it is almost impossible to grasp and fix it in a definition. Many have taken an entirely materialistic view of the matter, and attempted to measure it by the arithmetic of proportion or weigh it according to avoirdupois. Brantôme, one of the most decided of these, has the presumption to count on the ends of his fingers the qualities of female beauty, as if they were so many points in a fine horse. He enumerates them thus:

"Three white things—the skin, teeth, and hands.
Three dark—the eyes, eyebrows, and eyelids.
Three red—the lips, cheeks, and nails.
Three long—the body, hair, and hands.
Three short—the teeth, ears, and feet.
Three broad—the chest, forehead, and space between the eyes," etc., etc., etc.

Women are too apt to regard delicacy, in its physical sense of weakness, as an essential element of beauty. This is a false and dangerous notion, which finds expression in the affectation of paleness of complexion and tenuity of figure, which are deliberately acquired by a systematic disobedience of the laws of health. No unwholesome person, whatever may be the regularity of her features and the fineness of her mould, can justly claim to be beautiful; and we doubt whether any woman who cultivates sickness and weakness has a sound idea of the value of good looks.

There can be no beauty without health; and it might also be said that there can not be health without beauty. Form, color, and expression are essentially dependent upon the soundness of the human structure for their attractiveness. The grace of a justly-proportioned stature and well-moulded limbs can only be the result of wholesome bone and flesh. The skeleton must be composed of a substance in which certain mineral and animal matters are mixed in fixed proportions, or it will neither possess the flexibility nor the firmness necessary to the erectness combined with mobility proper to the human figure. Too much or too little of either ingredient not only indicates disease, but is fatal to beauty of form. Those human monsters of dwarfed proportions and devious shape, occasionally seen, owe their ugliness to a want of mineral matter, or lime, in their bones. These, being deficient in stiffness, are unable to resist the wanton action of the muscles, and are thus cramped, twisted, and knotted into a tangled heap of deformity. So a too meagre supply of animal matter, or oil, another proof of disease, will give the bony frame an inflexibility and brittleness fatal to ease and grace of movement. This unctuousness is apt to evaporate with the coming of disappointment, the exhaustion of strength, and advance of time, and thus the primness of the old maid and bachelor, and rigidity of the patriarch.

The contour of the human figure derives its principal beauty from the soft parts which cover and are contained within the bony frame. The muscles must be originally endowed with strength and continually invigorated by exercise in order that they may have that graduated fullness and waviness of outline essential to a beautiful form. Spread over the muscles, and penetrating between them, are layers of fat and cellular tissue, which, if in proper quantity, contribute not a little to external beauty. Any excess or deficiency, however, will be sure to result in ugliness. There is no hope of the prize of beauty being adjudged to the unduly bloated or collapsed of body, whatever may be the force of their pretensions in other respects. Excessive fatness or thinness is not only a deviation from the lines of proportion, but from the laws of health.

The lungs, the liver, the stomach, and entrails all bear a proportionate share in giving shape to the human structure. These organs must have that degree of development essential to health in order to fill up their proper places in the contour of the human form. If the lungs collapse from want of exercise, disease, or any other cause, the chest falls in, and loses the arched fullness of its natural beauty. If the stomach, liver, and entrails are, by excess and perverted use, forced into undue prominence, there results that deviation from natural proportion the most fatal to good looks, the pot-belly.

The condition of the blood has also much to do with human beauty or ugliness. This fluid of life must have certain ingredients, and those only mixed in certain proportions, or it will not have the qualities essential either to good health or looks. A want of one of its smaller constituents, iron, will deprive the blood not only of its strength, but its color, and thus the person in whose veins it circulates will be in danger, as he will have the pallor of death. When some substance gets into the blood which should not be there, it not only poisons, but discolors the body.

Thus, in a case of jaundice, the whole skin will be stained with an ugly tint varying from yellow to green.

The condition of the skin, which is the envelope of the whole human structure, has a wonderful influence upon the external aspect. It is, as it were, the atmosphere which surrounds that microcosm, or little world, of human being—Man. Upon its purity depends greatly the look of every part and feature, which can only be seen through it. If the skin is not kept in a wholesome condition by a proper diet and regimen, there can be no beauty. A dingy integument will spoil the grace of proportion and delicacy of line of the most regularly cut face and perfectly moulded form.

It is useless for the naturally beautiful to attempt to preserve their charms while neglecting the care of their health; but wholesomeness is so satisfactory and attractive that its possessor needs no other quality to secure admiration and happiness.

Exercise in the open air, regular meals of nutritious food, daily bathing in cold water, and agreeable and systematic occupation, are the main requisites for giving health, strength, and grace to the human body.

The chief faults of the American person are

excessive paleness or yellowness of complexion, and thinness of structure. It is common for foreigners to praise our people for their good looks, and the American face is certainly remarkable for its regularity. It seldom presents those extraordinary deviations from the classical ideal so frequently observed in foreigners. Those monstrous developments of the features, which are not seldom found in the German or Irish countenance, and approximate it to the various types of the lower animals, are rare among native-born Americans. As people of all nations come hither, we have, of course, every kind of face. There are, accordingly, all varieties of disproportion and degrees of ugliness to be occasionally seen. These, such as the low heads and crumpled faces which look as if they had been squashed in the making; the nasal appendages fleshy and pendent like abortive elephants' trunks; the ears tumid and misshapen as gigantic oysters; the thick lips, eviscerated mouths, and projecting under jaws, are generally of foreign importation.

The American complexion is surpassed in freshness and clearness by the English in youth. Our dry atmosphere is unfavorable both to the color and transparency of the skin. In advanced age, however, we have decidedly the advantage. While the English complexion is apt to become pimpled and blowsy, and seems to indicate grossness and overfeeding, the American, with the progress of time, ripens to a mellow ruddiness, which harmonizes well with gray hairs, and the veneration which is due to them.

The American face, having generally but little fat or cellular tissue, shrinks readily into wrinkles, and thus we are supposed to wear out earlier than we do. The earnestness and activity of mind in the United States give a concentration to the expression of the general countenance, and also soon furrow it. Compare the peasant face of Europe with that of the working people of this country. The former appears like a mass of dough rolled into a uniform surface; the latter is full of lines, distinct and expressive as those of a steel engraving.

The pallidness of complexion and meagreness of frame which are characteristic of our women may be partly attributed to their diet, which is ordinarily not sufficiently generous to give ruddiness of color and fullness of flesh.

Our dames, although we do not advise them to go to bed nightly on a supper of Stilton cheese and London stout like their English sisters, would, we believe, improve their looks if they lived better. By living better we mean feeding at regular intervals upon well-cooked, nutritious food, instead of wasting their appetites upon cakes, sweets, and other indigestible articles, which fill the stomach, but starve the body. Hear what Brillat Savarin says upon the effects of good living: "*Gourmandise* is favorable to beauty. A train of exact and rigid observations have demonstrated that a succulent, delicate, and careful regimen repels to a distance, and for a length of time, the external appearance of old age. It gives more brilliancy to the eyes, more freshness to the skin, more support to the muscles; and as it is certain in physiology that it is the depression of the muscles which causes wrinkles, those formidable enemies of beauty, it is equally true to say that, *cæteris paribus*, those who understand eating are comparatively ten years younger than those who are strangers to this science."

The necessity of frequent bathing, not only for the preservation of health, but of beauty, is apparent from the structure and functions of the skin. This is divided by anatomists into two layers, the epidermis and dermis. The former is the most external, and is called sometimes the scarf-skin. This is being constantly formed anew, while the old gathers upon the surface in heaps of scales, which are more or less adherent. If allowed to accumulate, they will seriously injure not only the health of the skin itself, but that of the whole body. They will irritate the surface, producing various ugly eruptions, dull the sensibility, and destroy the gloss, flexibility, and transparency upon which the beauty of the complexion and skin especially depends. These will, moreover, if left to increase and harden, so close up the pores as to hinder the transpiration essential to health and life.

The only effectual means of getting rid of these deposits is by the use of soap. The scales of the scarf-skin are composed of albumen, the same as the white of eggs, and this is soluble in what the chemists term alkalies. Now soaps of all kinds, containing as their principal constituent potash or soda, which are chemically described as alkalies, are, according to science as well as experience, the best cleansers of the skin, for they dissolve the natural scarf, as well as the oil which accumulates upon it. Thus, while removing dirt from the body, we are performing at the same time a function necessary to health.

It is said of a Frenchwoman that she once remarked, "How strange it is that we should be always washing our hands, when we never wash our feet!" It is to be hoped that this strangeness was peculiar to herself. A no less remarkable fact, however, and one which is unquestionably so general as to justify an observation, is the limited application of soap to the human body. Without extending our inquiry beyond the face, let us ask how many fair dames ever apply a lather to their complexions? Now we advise them to overturn into the fire all their face-washes, as the good Vicar of Wakefield did those of his daughters, and to betake themselves to soap. The best kind should be used, such as the well-known Windsor, or any other in which the alkali is not too abundant or strong. The ordinary cosmetics and artificial washes hide, but do not cleanse away the dirt, and are apt, moreover, to mottle the complexion with brown and yellow spots,* like the eyes of grease in an ill-made soup.

Under the outer covering, or epidermis, is the thicker dermis, or sensitive skin. The ruddy color observed in the healthy of our race comes from the blood circulating in this inner layer of the human integument. This is beyond the reach of the paint-pot and face-washes; and there is no other means of preserving its beautiful roseate tint, and giving full effect to its brilliancy in the complexion, than by a proper care—with

* We shall so far indulge our fair readers as to tell them that lime-juice will remove these ugly stains, while at the same time reminding them that it will only take effect after a good preliminary lathering of the face.

suitable exercise, diet, and regimen—of the bodily health. It is from this inner source that comes the rose-blush which warms the pellucid whiteness of the blonde, and gives the ruddy mellowness of the peach to the ripe color of the brunette. That, however, it may glow with all its natural purity and beauty, it is necessary that the thin veil which covers it should be kept unobstructed and translucent. If the scarf, or outer skin, becomes thickened and dulled by neglect, dirt, and the use of cosmetics, the color of the inner, or sensitive skin, will necessarily be hidden, and the chief charm of the natural complexion of our race lost. A proper attention to the general health, and a free use of soap and water all over, are the only means of obtaining a sound skin and a good complexion.*

* Ever since a traveler imprudently revealed the fact that some women, of the Carpathian valleys, we believe, secured for themselves beautiful complexions by feeding on arsenic, this practice, it is said, has been more or less generally adopted, not only in Europe, but in this country. Physicians have, moreover, for a long time been in the habit of prescribing, in diseases of the skin, a preparation called *Fowler's Solution*, the principal constituent of which is arsenic. This remedy is considered an effective one, but its danger is so great that it is given only in the smallest doses, and its operation is watched with the utmost care and anxiety. Arsenic is one of the deadliest poisons, and no one should venture, with the remote possibility of its giving clearness to the complexion, to dabble with it.

CHAPTER III.

Relation of Dress to Form.—The Hair.—Dyes.—Grayness.—Hair-cutting.—Its Effect.—The Nose.—The Eye.—Squinting.—Short-sightedness.—Eyebrows and Eyelashes.—The morbid Phase of Fashion.—Dark-rimmed Eyes.

WHILE in ancient times it was the form which gave shape to the dress, nowadays it is the dress which gives shape to the form. We have thus given up our bodies to the tailor and dress-maker to be fashioned according to their caprices. The Greek woman, with a genuine contour of swelling bosom and rounded limb, was content to cover herself with a simple cloth, which, confident in her graceful proportions, she left to assume the natural lines of her figure. The modern dame of fashion, distrustful of nature, resorts to the artifices of the dress-maker, and thus, with no visible sign of her original form, breathes, sighs, and swells in depths of cotton and circumferences of whalebone.

Though the "lady" and "gentleman" of our day, being lay figures more or less stuffed with hair and stiffened with wire, have little to do with their general "make-up," there are certain parts of their bodies which they can not wholly disguise with the shams of dress. These, therefore, remain more or less in their natural state, and are left to show the beauties or defects they may possess. Of such parts of their bodies men and women are not in the habit of delegating the entire care to other hands than their own. While, therefore, we do not presume to meddle with the mantua-maker and tailor, but leave to their art the skillful disposition of the lines and proportions of the human figure, we shall venture to claim for nature a part in the management of those portions of the frame which can not be wholly concealed or disguised.

There is no part of the human body with which the busy hand of fashion has so much interfered as the hair, and especially that of woman. Female ingenuity seems exhaustless of device in twisting, plaiting, frizzing, knotting, heaping up, scattering, and torturing into every possible form and direction the flexible material which naturally covers the head. Of these multiform monstrosities of shape there is none uglier than the chignon, lately so prevalent and still lingering unfortunately. This tumor-like excrescence disfigures the top of the head with the appearance of a horrid growth of disease which would seem to call for the knife of the surgeon did we not know that it could be placed or displaced at the will of the wearer—sufferer we were about to say.*

We are grateful to modern fashion for its tasteful rejection of the front of false hair, and the graceful submission of old age to its whitened locks. There is no severer trial of reverence than the sight of one of those ugly patches of black stuck over the eyes of a matron, and nothing can accord so ill as its positiveness of color and precision of outline with the mottled mellowness and wavy lines of an aged face.

Dyeing the hair is the most preposterous of all attempts at human deceit; for it deceives no one but the deceiver himself, whose vanity leads him to believe that his artifice is successful. There is no one who has once commenced this practice of giving an artificial color to his hair

* The hair of which the *chignon* or *waterfall* is made is mostly brought from Caffreland, where it is cut from the heads of the filthiest and most disgusting population in the world. The former sources of supply, the peasants of Germany, and the dead of hospitals and prisons, are incapable of furnishing the excessive demand for hair created by the general prevalence of the present monstrosity of fashion. The Hottentot product is shipped to London, near which there is a place where it was purified. This, however, in consequence of the intolerable stench, has been indicted as a nuisance.

but must regret it. It is generally begun with the idea that a single application will be sufficient for all time; but when it is discovered that it must be continued, the constant repetition of the dirty and fatiguing process soon becomes wearisome and disgusting. Each application of the dye, whatever it may be, colors, or discolors rather, only that portion of the hair above the surface of the scalp. The new growth, which is constantly taking place from the roots, appears always with the natural tint.

There is a premature grayness which sometimes occurs in the young, chiefly in those of light complexions and light-colored hair, which is the consequence of weakness of the nervous power. This, as well as the loosening and falling out of the hair, which come often from the same cause, may be checked by increase of the general vigor and the use of proper local remedies. A useful practice, when the hair is sufficiently short to admit of it, is to plunge the head in cold water morning and night, and, after thoroughly drying, to brush it briskly until the scalp is warmed to a glow. A simple lotion composed of half an ounce of vinegar of cantharides, and an ounce each of Cologne and rose waters, rubbed on the scalp, will probably be found beneficial. The dandruff, which is a natural formation composed of the scales of the skin which are being constantly thrown off, requires only a proper cleanliness to prevent its too great accumulation, and a moderate use of oil or pomatum to moisten the scalp.

It is very questionable whether frequent cutting of the hair is as favorable to its growth and beauty as is generally supposed. In fact, some of the most luxuriant heads of hair we have ever seen had never been touched by the scissors. It is quite certain that the common practice of cropping, or shaving the head for the purpose of strengthening the growth of the hair, not only fails of this effect, but often produces the contrary result, and not seldom total baldness ensues where a small stock is sacrificed with the delusive hope of obtaining a great supply.

The depilatories of the nostrum venders for the removal of superfluous hair are dangerous. If dame or damsel should be troubled by the show of a mustache or beard, we know of no means of checking this masculine encroachment but by the patient use of the tweezers.

The American Indians are said to succeed in smoothing their faces by persistingly plucking out each hair as it grows.

There is no feature of the face so essential to good looks as the nose. It admits of great variety of form, but it must be there in some shape or other. Though the nose is not capable, as the eye and mouth, of much variety of expression, its particular conformation has more to do than that of any other single feature with the individual character of the human countenance. Change this in a drawing, without altering any other part, and you will find with each variety a complete transformation of the whole face.

The Grecian nose, with its straight lines and symmetrical arrangement, has been generally accepted by artists as the most beautiful; but different nations, notwithstanding, cling fondly to their own particular forms of this organ. A Hottentot Venus, we may be assured, would never receive the prize of beauty from any Paris of her own race if she were destitute of the national flat nose. Sir Joshua Reynolds, who held that the idea of beauty was dependent upon the association of ideas, would evidently have approved of the principles of the African judge. He would, however, at the same time have congratulated himself, doubtless, that, being an Englishman, he was not bound to accept the flat nose of Ethiopia as a necessary element of his own idea of beauty. "I suppose nobody will doubt," he says, "if a negro painter was to paint the Goddess of Beauty, that he would represent her black, with thick lips, flat nose, and woolly hair; and it seems to me that he would act very unnaturally if he did not; for by what criterion will any one dispute his idea?"

There seems to be no absolute standard of nasal beauty. The Romans were proud of their stern and portentous aquilines, and the Israelites would probably not be content to lose the smallest tip of their redundant beaks. The Tartars, having no noses to speak of, affect to consider the deficiency a beauty. The wife of Genghis Khan was esteemed the most charming woman in all Tartary because she only had two holes where her nose should have been.

The peculiar form of the nose seems in fact to have but little influence upon our likes and dislikes. Mirabeau, who had a nose as widespread as that of a Hottentot, and Gibbon and Wilkes, whose noses were reduced to barely perceptible snubs, were very successful suitors of the female sex. The turn-up nose can not be justified by any principle of taste, and yet the *nez retroussé*, by which French appellation we are fond of dignifying the pug, is so far from diminishing, that it seems to increase the admiration of man for the woman who possesses it. No heroine of a modern novel appears complete without the *nez retroussé*, and Madame Du Barri, the common town courtesan, owes to it her place in history by the side of the worthless Louis XV.

There is no part of the physiognomy which reveals so quickly and clearly ill temper and bad habits as the nose. Every snarling, discontented, proud, and envious emotion is accompanied by a lifting of the end of each nostril through the agency of a little muscle, which, after frequent action, gives to the nose a permanent turn-up, which is as repulsive as the snout of an ill-tempered dog. The nose, moreover, like the door-post of an old-fashioned inn, scores every excess of eating and drinking, and so prominently as to be read by the passer-by.*

* The nose, as is well known, is the organ of smell. For this purpose it is endowed with a pair of nerves, called the olfactory, whose abounding filaments pierce the many holes and cover the multiple surfaces of the light and porous structure termed the spongy bone, which lies at the root of each nostril. This peculiar organization is with the object of giving free entrance to the air, through the medium of which odor is conveyed to the nerve, in which the sense of smell resides. The act of smelling is performed by closing the mouth and breathing through the nostrils, which expand to the odorous gale which thus enters and is diffused through every opening and over each surface of the bone where the nerve penetrates and expands its closely-woven net of threads. Man is naturally endowed with an acute sense of smell, but its power can be greatly increased or diminished by art. Those whose vocation is among stenches become by practiced indifference almost regardless of them; and others, whose busi-

The eye is, above all, the glory of the face. With it we chiefly express our reverential subordination to the Deity, and our familiar relations with man; see visions of divine beauty in nature, and catch that light of sympathy by which we recognize in every human countenance a brother.

The eye is especially a social feature, and it becomes us, therefore, more particularly to guard and use it with a discreet care. Its beauty, whatever may be its natural character, is greatly dependent upon the general health. Any thing which tends to weaken the powers of the body affects more or less the condition of the eye.

ness requires a discriminating nicety of the sense, obtain by studied attention a marvelous acuteness of smell. There was a night-man in Berlin who declared that he was not sensible of the intensest smell of his odoriferous occupation. On the examination of his body after death no olfactory nerve was found. Whether this was an original defect, or only the result of a long and resolute disuse of his sense of smell, could not be determined. Nature or art had made him the right man for the right place. The dog and some other animals have a much acuter sense of smell than man, and we accordingly find in them larger olfactory nerves, and more extensive, porous, and convoluted spongy bones for the exposure of their filaments to the odorous breath of the air. A dog, by the sense of smell, will trace and nose out his master in the most multitudinous crowd. This proves not only the acuteness of the smelling power of the animal, but establishes the fact that each man, as well as every race of men, has a peculiar odor.

Excess of all kinds is reflected in it at once, and it is doubtful whether any abuse of the organ itself, apart from the application of direct violence, is so injurious as the inordinate indulgence of the passions, or the practice of those habits which enervate and finally destroy the human constitution.

Short-sightedness is not always, as it is often supposed, a natural defect. It is frequently acquired by the habit in youth of applying the eyes too closely to the object of vision. Thus it is not an infrequent result of the practice common among children of bending their heads too near to the books they read. This fatal habit should be carefully guarded against by parents. Even where there seems to be a natural defect, it will often yield to a proper regimen of the eyes. Modern oculists reject the old idea that it is good for short-sighted people to make constant efforts to see without artificial aid. Now it is held to be a judicious proceeding to resort as early as possible to the use of glasses, which should be adapted precisely to the wants of the person. These are only to be recognized by a patient trial under the direction of an adept in the art.

Squinting is another defect often attributed to Nature, when it is not seldom due to a willful neglect of its laws. Surgeons have abandoned the operation for this deformity, and as the knife has proved useless in eradicating the evil when formed, it behooves all to be more careful to prevent its formation. Among the frequent causes of this ugly defect are some so slight that they are seldom noticed by those who have the care of the young. An ill-fitting cap or bonnet, with a too projecting front, or a loose ribbon or tape falling from above and dangling within the field of vision, is often the commencing cause of a squint. It is not seldom produced, also, by neglecting to have the child's hair cut, which, consequently, is allowed to hang down and shake loosely above the eyes, which are thus frequently and irregularly diverted, until their sight becomes permanently cross.

The eyebrows and lashes can not be much interfered with to their advantage by art. The regularity and smoothness of the hairs, which are essential to the beauty of the brow, are undoubtedly favored by occasional rubbing or brushing in a uniform direction with a fine cloth or soft brush. A solution of sulphate of quinine has been recommended as a useful application to thin eyebrows. Shaving these or the lashes is a pernicious practice, and, so far from improving either, will result in a perverse, if any, growth at all of new hair.

Some people, whose two eyebrows have a tendency to unite, are so uneasy at it that they persistently pluck out the approaching hairs. It may console such to know that such a union was esteemed a beauty by the ancients; and Tennyson alludes to this peculiar growth, which was common to his friend Hallam and to Michael Angelo, in these, to many incomprehensible. lines:

> "And over thine ethereal eyes
> The *bar* of Michael Angelo."

The eyelashes, which, to be eminently beautiful, should be long and deeply black, are dependent greatly upon the general health and the condition of the organs which they adorn and protect for their good appearance. Any thing which directly fatigues the eye, or indirectly affects it by weakening the body, is sure to show its mark upon the edges of the eyelids. These become more or less inflamed, reddened, saturated with tears, and besmeared with a mucous which, thickening and hardening about their roots, finally detaches them. The scales or crusts thus formed should never be torn away with violence, for the hairs are sure to come with them. The best mode of removing them is to apply at night a little cold cream to the edges of the lids of the closed eye, and in the morning to bathe them with lukewarm milk and water. When these incrustations become inveterate, means must be taken to strengthen the general health. The best local application is the slightest touch of dilute citrine ointment.

Nothing is worse for the eyes than straining them to see with an imperfect light, and every one who cares to preserve their strength and beauty should avoid using them in the uncertain glimmer of twilight, or in the flicker of a sputtering tallow candle or ill-trimmed lamp. It may be well to remind our sentimental readers that all unnecessary weeping had better be avoided, for the delights of crying over the jilted Augustus or the broken-hearted Araminta of the last novel can not be indulged in without risk to the health and beauty of the eyes.

There is a phase of fashion which the doctors might call the *morbific*, characterized by an affectation of the symptoms of disease. The younger Dumas, with his phthisical heroines, as unsound in flesh as in morals, is greatly responsible for the vogue given to the pallid, wan, hectic, and feeble. We thus find the florid and robust assuming ill health when they have it not, and resorting to all kinds of contrivances to give the face a cast of sickliness, to which a robust nature has imparted her own freshness and brightness of color. Among the various expedients for giving themselves this fashionable "languishing, dying" air, that of darkening with a black pigment the orbit of the eye is in common use by many women. They thus produce a very fair imitation of what the French call *les yeux cernés*, and at certain distances the effect is not unlike that which is intended, but which we would suppose no delicate woman would care to exhibit so ostentatiously.

It is sometimes the practice to paint the eyebrows and eyelashes, and even to cloud the eyeballs by means of ink dropped between the lids.

Not only does a decorous taste emphatically condemn these practices, which give unmistakable indications of the painted Jezebel, but prudence forbids them. All pigments, even when applied to the surface of the surrounding parts of the eye, are dangerous, and nothing like ink can be dropped upon that delicate organ without certain mischief. We know of a permanent loss of sight from paralysis produced by the frequent use of belladonna to give an unnatural largeness to the pupil, supposed to be, by some women of a morbid taste, a sign of languishing beauty.

CHAPTER IV.

The Ear.—How to make it beautiful.—Ear-wax.—Ear-pulling.—The Mouth.—Its Beauty and Ugliness.—The Proud Muscle.—The Tongue.—Tongue-scraping.—The Teeth.—Proper Management.—Use of Tobacco.

The human ear in its more perfect forms is certainly a beautiful object; but there is no feature which is so frequently unattractive. This may be owing to its neglect in childhood and youth. Being round the corner, as it were, of the face, it is apt to be left uncared for, while the front is more diligently tended. The shape of the ear is generally deformed in infancy and childhood by the carelessness of mother or nurse. In adjusting the cap, hat, or bonnet, while every effort is made to give it as jaunty a setting as possible upon the head, with the due rakishness of inclination to the right or left, the ears are allowed to shift as they may for themselves. They thus are either crumpled up and pressed down irregularly under the tight rim of the covering of the head, or squeezed out from their natural resting-places, and forced into a stuck-out position which is by no means graceful. The careful mother will take the precaution, each time that she puts on the cap, hat, or bonnet, as it may be, to smooth down with her gentle hands the ears of her child, and see that they are held with a slight pressure, in their proper position, at the sides of the head, where they ought to snugly nestle. She will thus probably secure for her offspring a pair of small, transparent, delicately colored, and thin, shell-shaped ears such as Nature intended, and escape those monstrous productions we so often see, which have been likened, with more or less justness of comparison, to swollen, overripe purple figs, gigantic oysters, and asinine excrescences.

We can not but protest against the prevailing style of dressing the hair, which, violently drawn away from the ears, leaves them exposed in all their ugly nakedness. In the ancient Greek statue of female beauty the ear is always partially hidden by the hair. If, in its ideal grace, it modestly half retires from the sight, it certainly, in its modern matter-of-fact ugliness, should conceal itself altogether. We might possibly be persuaded to make an exception in favor of a beautiful ear, but we can not be prevailed upon to accept the exposure of the auricular monstrosities to be beheld every where. Do with them what you please, but keep them out of sight, or, at any rate, do not force their ugliness upon our notice by jingling or glistening gewgaws.

The ear is a most complicated and delicate apparatus; but, fortunately, it is so shut up within the casket of the skull that it can hardly be disarranged by our negligence or interference. It has over the openings of its outer to the inmost of its series of winding passages membranes tightly stretched, like the parchment of a drum, and these vibrate to every sound, which is conveyed from one to the other by a chain of little bones. These, in turn, transmit the vibration to threads of nerves, which communicate the sensation to the brain, and enable the mysterious power of this organ to form a perception of sound. As in the case of the military drum, the membranes of the ear, which in fact are called drums, require for their proper vibration the presence of air on both sides. This, in case of the ear, is provided for not only by its external opening, but by an internal communication with the mouth and nose. Hence any cause which closes these inlets to the atmosphere is sure to affect the hearing. Thus an ordinary cold in the head, which swells the membrane of the nostrils, augments their natural discharge, and stuffs them up, as it were, always produces a certain degree of deafness. The outer opening to the ear secretes for its protection, and to keep the passage smooth for the conveyance of sound, a natural wax. This is apt to accumulate in undue quantity, become hardened, and produce deafness and a disagreeable ringing sound. A little warm water squeezed into the ear from a sponge, and a drop or two of sweet oil let fall into it afterward, will generally remove the accumulation. If not, recourse should be had to the surgeon, who with a syringe and a blunt instrument will soon get rid of the uncomfortable deposit. It is a dangerous practice for persons to be fumbling about their ears with the ordinary little steel spoon at the end of the tweezers found in most dressing-cases. If thrust too far and forcibly into the ear, it may penetrate or tear its external drum and seriously damage the hearing. Most of the cases of prolonged deafness arise from permanent destruction of the internal apparatus or paralysis of the nerves of the ear, and are unfortunately beyond the reach of art. These are the incurable cases upon which the quack speculates with such pecuniary success. His impudent and lying assertion of power never fails to find a credulous ear among those who have turned away in despair from the honest confession of impotency of the man of science.

Ear-pulling of all kinds, whether in fun or

earnest, practiced condescendingly or magisterially, by an emperor in his good, or by a schoolmaster in his bad humors, is ungracious and dangerous. Children's ears are thus frequently injured, and always distorted, if the pulling is habitual.

As far as appearance is concerned, it does not matter much what shape the male mouth may have, as, with the present style of wearing the mustache and beard, little of it can be seen. In the smooth face of woman, however, the form of the mouth has a great deal to do with its beauty or ugliness. The standard of taste in regard to this, as to other features, varies in different nations. The African not only prefers the flat nose, but the blubber lip; and Mungo Park, when traveling on the banks of the Niger, overheard a conclave of negro native matrons discussing the possibility of there being in any part of the world a woman capable of kissing such a shriveled mouth as his European one. Frightful, however, as were his thin lips, this did not prevent the African maiden from moistening them in their agony of fevered thirst with a draught of water from her refreshing gourd. Such was the triumph of woman's tenderness that it even overcame her natural disgust.

Though we are far from admiring the African

mouth, we consider a certain fullness of the lips essential to female loveliness. The thin lip, making no show of a ruddy succulence, seems to indicate, with a meagreness and acridity of blood, a cold and sour disposition; and we are not surprised to read that the shrewish Xantippe, the incompatible spouse of Socrates, was lean-mouthed.

The most lovable of mouths is given to the bride by Suckling in his *Ballad on a Wedding:*

> "Her lips were red, and one was thin
> Compared to that was next her chin,
> Some bee had stung it newly."

All the poets—and they are supposed to have the nicest sensibility to female as to other beauty—agree in bestowing a certain fullness and redness upon the lips of their ideal loves. The expanding rose-bud is, as is well known, the traditional comparison:

> "Roses are her cheeks,
> And a rose her mouth."

The more the line of the upper lip resembles the form of the classical bow, the more closely it approaches the ideal of beauty. This potent weapon of Apollo and Cupid, in fact, was modeled from the curve of the mouth, and symbolizes, in the eloquence of the one and the love of the other, the power of words, whether whispered in the ear of affection or thundered forth to the hearing of a multitude.

There is no art potent enough to give the beauty of symmetry which Nature may have refused to the lips. If they become unnaturally pale, more or less *rouge* mixed with beeswax will give them a deceitful and temporary gloss of nature. To this daubing our fashionable dames are constantly obliged to resort, for their exhausting lives of dissipation impoverish and decolorize the blood, and the effect is apparent at once in the blanched lip. A frequent usage, however, of the lip salve, as it is ingeniously called, but which is merely a red pigment in disguise, so inflames, thickens, roughens, and gives such a peculiar tint to the mouth, that it has the look of the shriveled, purplish one of a sick negress.* The habit of biting the lips soon destroys any grace of form they may have originally possessed. Madame de Pompadour, while lamenting the decay of her charms, confessed that she first began to spoil at the mouth. She had early acquired the habit of biting her lips in order to conceal her emotion. "At thirty years," says a historian, "her mouth had lost all its striking brilliancy." She, too, began at a very early

* The best wash to give a pleasant taste to the mouth and odor to the breath is a weak infusion of mint.

period to touch herself up with that paint so fatal to the duration of facial charms, and at court only dared to show herself by candle-light.

The mouth, supplied with a number of muscles quick to act at the vaguest command of the will, is very expressive of the disposition. There is one little one against whose action we would put our young damsels on their guard. It is the same as that which turns up the nostril at the least emotion of pride, envy, or disgust. It also at the same time, for it is connected with the mouth, pulls up its upper lip. The effect of the frequent exercise of all muscles of the face is to give a permanent expression according to the direction of their action. This is more marked in that of the mouth and nose, called by the ancients the *musculus superbus*, or proud muscle. If our pretty girls desire to grow old gracefully, we would advise them to be chary of the use of this telltale messenger, for, if his services should be often availed of, he will be sure to turn up the nose and lip in permanent disgust of his functions. It is the most distinctive and repulsive sign of an envious old maid or any other ill-tempered person.

Whatever beauty of form and grace of proportion the human tongue may have, no one but the possessor is supposed to be cognizant of them.

People are not in the habit of thrusting out this organ to the gaze of others except in illness for the inspection of the doctor, or in rudeness, to express contempt of an opponent.

The tongue, however, though not wont to make a frequent appearance before the public, demands no less care for the proper performance of the duties of its private station. Upon its surface there is apt to gather a fur which is not easily removed by the ordinary rinsing of the mouth. There is an instrument of silver, called a tongue-scraper, which was never absent from the toilette-cases of our grandams, but is now almost obsolete, that is well adapted to this purpose, and should be used every morning to remove the covering of thickened mucus which accumulates in the course of the night. This fur, if left, gives a sensation of pastiness and fullness to the mouth, and not only destroys the delicacy of the taste and the disposition for food, but thickens the voice.

Dr. Holmes, in one of his medical essays, gives an historical importance to the tongue-scraper. "I," says he, "think more of this little implement on account of its agency in saving the colony at Plymouth in the year 1623. Edward Winslow heard that Massasoit was sick and like to die. He found him with a houseful of people about him, women rubbing his arms and legs, and friends 'making such a hellish noise' as they probably thought would scare away the devil of sickness. Winslow gave him some conserve, washed his mouth, *scraped his tongue*, which was in a horrid state, got down some drink, made him some broth, dosed him with an infusion of strawberry leaves and sassafras root, and had the satisfaction of seeing him rapidly recover. Massasoit, full of gratitude, revealed the plot which had been formed to destroy the colonists, whereupon the governor ordered Captain Miles Standish to see to it." The captain did effectually "see to it," and stabbing Peckswot, the ringleader, with his own knife, broke up the plot and saved the colony.

The old-fashioned doctor is apt to trust too much to the tongue as an indicator of the state of the stomach, and has often recourse to a severe drench of the remote organ, where a simple scrape of the near and tangible one would be more effectual. A mere fur of the tongue should alarm no one, if unaccompanied by no other indication of disease; for, in nine cases out of ten, it is only a local foulness, easily removed by the scraper, or destined quickly to disappear through the natural self-cleansing of the mouth.

The tongue, though its recuperative power is

very great and rapid, as is proved by the quickness and completeness with which a cut, a blister, or a burn, or any ordinary injury of it will heal, may become the seat of serious disease by prolonged irritation. Thus a jagged tooth, the continued pressure of the pipe-stem, and the end of the cigar, will produce tedious ulcers of the tongue, and occasionally deadly cancers.

The tongue has the exclusive credit for functions that do not belong to it. It is not either the sole organ of language or of taste. The throat, with its vocal chords and its palate, and the nose, with its nerves and its air-passages, have a large and indispensable share both in tasting and talking.

The tongue is ordinarily the most abused of all the organs of sense. While the eye and the ear merely suffer from neglect, the tongue is laboriously perverted. Its nature, by the persistent diligence of a malevolent art, is so totally changed that its dislikes become likes, and its likes dislikes. Tobacco, at first spat out with infinite disgust, is finally fondled with delight by the enslaved tongue, and the simple food of nature is rejected for the spiced dishes of art.

The tongue, it must be confessed, as the organ of material taste, has no very dignified function, and has reason to withdraw itself from public notice. It has been likened to a commissary general, whose supplies are necessary to the action of the other more noble organs, but whose sword is seldom drawn, while its aspect is by no means heroic.

The mouth, however distorted its form or preposterous its size, if it only shows a range of sound and clean teeth, can scarcely be deemed ugly. There is a wholesomeness of look in a row of pure white ivories, set regularly in a rim of ruddy coral, which reconciles the observer to an otherwise unprepossessing face.

A wholesome condition of the teeth is not only essential to good looks, but to daily comfort and permanent health. Chewing of the food, so necessary to a good digestion, can not be properly performed with weak and diseased masticators, which are, in fact, the frequent cause of dyspepsia and other affections of the stomach. Local diseases of the most tormenting kind, such as *tic douloureux* and the various painful face, head, and ear aches, and disorders of the eye, as well as the fatal cancer and tedious ulcers of the tongue and lips, are often due to no other cause than a decayed and ragged tooth.

Though the natural constitution of the body and the various accidental diseases to which it is liable may have something to do with the bad condition of the teeth, their ill looks and decay are generally owing to a neglect of cleanliness. The mischief is most frequently done at an early age. In childhood an indifference to personal appearance, with that disinclination to any effort which does not bring immediate pleasure, leads to a disregard of the teeth. This occurs just at the time when they require the greatest care. At about eleven years of age most of the permanent teeth have taken the place of those of infancy, which are called the *deciduous*, since they fall away or are absorbed to make room for others. At this period the child should be compelled to rub his teeth with a soft brush, and rinse his mouth after each meal. These simple means are all that are necessary to purify and preserve them, provided the child makes no other use of his teeth than that for which Nature intended them. The jaws were, of course, never designed for nut-crackers, and the attempt so to pervert their purpose must necessarily prove fatal to the teeth. Though no perceptible fracture may be the immediate result, the tooth undoubtedly receives from the shock of each crushed hickory a seriously damaging effect, either to the nerve, the socket, or the enameled surface which covers it. With due care of the teeth, begun in childhood and prolonged through life, any person may reasonably calculate upon a set, if not of handsome, of useful grinders, to the end of his threescore years and ten.

The decay of the teeth is generally owing to the action of the acids generated by the fermentation of the particles of food deposited between them and at their roots during eating. To prevent this, the obvious way is to remove these deposits after each meal. The French practice of handing round the toothpicks and mouth-rinsers at the close of every repast is a good one for the teeth, though offensive to the fastidiousness of our manners. All that we have to say here is, that the sooner the particles of food are picked out and washed away, the better. The fastidious Chesterfield even did not hesitate to send that son, whom he was striving so laboriously to lick into shape, "by way of New-year's gift, a very pretty toothpick-case."

People should be on their guard against the too busy fingers of the dentist, who ought not to be allowed to file and scrape the teeth merely for the purpose of giving them an artificial regularity and whiteness not bestowed by Nature. When there is actual decay, then, and not till then, should he be permitted to make a free use of his instruments. The tartar which is apt to gather at the root of the teeth can be kept away by diligent cleaning; but, if once allowed to accumulate and harden, it will become necessary to remove it with a metallic scraper. As a general thing, a brush and water, if used sufficiently often, will be all that are required for cleaning the teeth. The only article that can be added with safety is a little good soap, like the English Windsor.

We are sorry to find that it is the belief of some dentists that that vilest of nauseous habits, tobacco-chewing, is favorable to the preservation of the teeth. This has long been the apology of our Southern and Western dames for their foul but favorite practice of *dipping* or besmearing their gums and teeth with snuff. Whatever good tobacco may do directly to the teeth is more than counterbalanced by the indirect injury they receive from the bodily disorders produced by the excessive use of this popular weed.

There can be no question that much smoking is fatal, if not to the soundness of the teeth, to their good looks, as it stains them with an ashy, fuliginous color.

CHAPTER V.

The Hand.—Its Beauty and Utility.—How to beautify the Hand.—Care of the Nails.—Hang-nails.—Snapping of the Fingers.—Dangers of the Practice.—Warts.—Sweating of the Hands.—The Foot.—The proper Form of the Shoe.—The Defects of the fashionable Shoe.—Corns.—Bunions.—Ingrowth of the Nail.—A terrific Operation.—Sweating of the Feet.

Sir Charles Bell, the great surgeon and anatomist, was so impressed with the adaptation of the hand to the various uses of man, that he made it the subject of the "Bridgewater" treatise he was appointed to write. He could find no better proof of the manifestation of design on the part of the Creator throughout the whole human structure than in that small but most finished piece of mechanism. The hand is indeed the most serviceable as well as graceful instrument with which man is endowed. It works so obediently to the will of its master that there is nothing within the range of human power that it can not perform. It records indelibly the quickest flash of thought, and gives, in a deadly stroke, terrible expression to the rage of man.

Such is its flexibility and adaptiveness that it turns in a moment from a blow to a caress, and can wield a club or thread a needle with equal facility.

The hand can not only perform faithfully its own duties, but, when necessary, will act for other parts of the human frame. It reads for the blind, and talks for the deaf and dumb. Machinery itself is but an imitation of the human hand on an enlarged scale; and all the marvelous performances of the former are justly due to the latter. It thus not only thoroughly performs its natural task, but, having the rare quality of extending its powers, enlarges its scope of work almost indefinitely. With the steam-engine, made and worked by itself, the human hand executes wonders of skill and force; and with the electric telegraph it, by the gentlest touch, awakens in an instant the sentiment of the whole world and makes it kin.

"For the queen's hand," says an elegant writer, "there is the sceptre, and for the soldier's hand the sword; for the carpenter's hand the saw, and for the smith's hand the hammer; for the farmer's hand the plow; for the miner's hand the spade; for the sailor's hand the oar; for the painter's hand the brush; for the sculptor's hand the chisel; for the poet's hand the pen; and for the woman's hand the needle. If none of these or the like will fit us, the felon's chain should be round our wrist, and our hand on the prisoner's crank." The hand was undoubtedly made for work, and should be used in accordance with its design.

The labor of the hand, however, especially that of the lighter kind, which generally falls to the lot of woman, ought not to prevent a due attention to the preservation of all the grace and beauty with which Nature originally endowed it. The idea is prevalent that absolute smallness, without regard to proportion, is essential to the beauty of a woman's hand. This keeps many a young girl idle, lest by work it should become enlarged. The hand will undoubtedly increase in size by use; but, if it only grows in proportion to other parts of the body, so far from this being an ugliness, it will be, according to all the laws of taste, a beauty. Fashion alone can find grace in a female hand dwarfed of its proportions by depriving it of its natural exercise, and by pinching it with a too short and narrow glove. Nothing is uglier, except it be a Chinese club-foot, to our sight, than those cramped paws of kid in which our fashionable women delight. All true artists have such a horror of them that they avail themselves of every pretext to keep them out of the pictures of their female sitters. The pinching glove, as generally worn, is not only excessively uncomfortable, especially in cold weather, but it permanently deforms the hand, rendering it lumpy and podgy.

Much can be done by care to beautify the fingers, upon the grace of which depends greatly the beauty of the whole hand. The natural tapering length of these can only be preserved by removing from them all pinching manacles of kid and jewelry. Much of the beauty of the finger depends upon the proper treatment of the nails. These, if cut too close, deform the finger-ends and render them stubby. The upper and free border of the nail should always be left projecting a line or so beyond the extremity of the finger, and be pared only to a slight curve, without encroaching too much on the angles. To preserve the half moon, or what the anatomists call the *lunula*, which rises just above the root of the nail, and is esteemed so great a beauty, care must be taken to keep down the skin, which constantly tends to encroach upon it. This should be done with a blunt ivory instrument, and the growth gently pushed away, but never cut. By this means, also, the production of the annoying "hang-nail" will be prevented. The habit of filing or scraping the nails is fatal to their perfection, as it thickens their substance and destroys their natural transparency. The ordinary finger-brush should alone be used for cleaning and polishing the nails. It is a curious fact that Rousseau, in his *Confessions*, records the use of this simple instrument, now indispensable to every cleanly person, as proof of the excessive coxcombry of his friend, the courtly Grimm. Thus the luxury of one age becomes the necessity of another.

The ugly habit of biting the nails is fatal to their beauty. They become excessively brittle in consequence, not being allowed time to acquire their natural toughness, and, moreover, the ends of the fingers, being unsupported, turn over, forming an ugly rim of hard flesh, which will prevent the regular growth of the nail.

The not uncommon practice of *snapping* the fingers, as it is termed, is fatal to their good looks. It stretches and weakens the ligaments, and so enlarges the knuckles and joints that the whole hand becomes knotty and of a very unsightly appearance.

The wart is an ugly excrescence, but will generally disappear, especially from the hands of the young, without any interference. It is better patiently to await this result than to make use of the knife or the caustic. The safest of these means is the acetic acid, which may be applied gently with a camel's-hair pencil, once each day, to the summit of the wart. Care should be taken to prevent this or any other powerful acid or caustic which may be used from touching the surrounding skin. It may be well, for this purpose, to cover the parts about the root of the wart with wax during the application of the remedy.

There is a not uncommon affection of the hands, which the French might gently term an *incommodité*, or an inconvenience, but which is a serious annoyance to the afflicted. This is a moist condition, which seems to resist all the ordinary efforts of absorption. Such hands are so constantly dripping with humidity that every thing they wear or touch becomes readily saturated. The glove shows the effect at once in ugly stains, and the bare hand leaves a blur of dampness upon every surface with which it may come in contact. Nothing can be so disagreeable as a grasp with the over-moist hand.

This infirmity is not seldom constitutional, and, though difficult of eradication, may be greatly relieved. Whatever tends to strengthen the body will alleviate, if not entirely remedy, the excessive moisture of the hands. Exercise in the open air, cold bathing, a generous, but not too stimulating diet, habitual composure of mind, and perhaps a daily draught of some mineral water or medicinal dose containing iron, are the best general means of treatment. The most effective local applications are the juice of lemon and starch powder.

It may be doubted whether there exists throughout the whole civilized world a well-formed foot. Many exquisites of both sexes claim admiration for their pedal extremities, but it is the boots and shoes which cover them which we are called on to admire. Their feet, if bared, would present a very great divergence from the classical ideal of beauty. The firmly-planted foot, neither too large nor too small, but justly proportioned to the height and weight it sustains, the smooth surface and regularly-curved lines, the distinctness of the divisions and the perfect formation of each toe, with its well-marked separateness, and its gradation of size and regularity of detail to the very tip of the nail, are now to be seen only in art. In Greek nature they were found, for the ancient sandal, which left the foot unfettered, gave freedom to the development of its natural grace and proportions. The modern boot or shoe, with the prevalent notion that every thing must be sacrificed to smallness, has squeezed the foot into a lump as knotty and irregular as a bit of pudding-stone, where the distorted toes are so imbedded in the mass and mutilated by the pressure that it is impossible to pick them out in the individuality and completeness of their original forms.

The process of our dames hardly differs from that of the Chinese women, whose feet, from the early age of five years, are so firmly bandaged that, as they say themselves, they become dead. The extremity below the instep is forced into a line with the leg, and two of the toes are bent under the sole, and the whole kept in this unnatural and painful position by leathern thongs. "The Chinese women, rich and poor, are all," says the traveler Huc, "lame; at the extremity of their legs they have only shapeless stumps, always enveloped in bandages, and from which all the life has been squeezed out."

Young Chinese girls who have not been properly brought up, and acquired the accomplishment of lameness by means of a diligent torture of their feet from the earliest childhood, find it no easy matter to get married. This fashion of little feet is unquestionably most barbarous, absurd, and injurious to the development of the physical strength. "But what means," asks the despairing Huc, "are there of putting a stop to the deplorable practice? It is decreed by fashion, and who would dare to resist her dictates?" He thinks the Europeans have no right to be very severe upon the Chinese. We may say the same in regard to our American dames, for do they not daily torture and deform their feet with tight shoes, and resemble in this respect—with a difference only in degree—their goat-hoofed sisters of the Flowery Kingdom?

As our coarse climate forbids the sandal, and renders the shoe necessary, care should be taken to adapt it as perfectly as possible to the natural conformation of the foot. It should be long and wide enough to admit of a free play of the toes; the space between the heel and sole of the shoe should be firm, and of a curve of the same height as the natural arch of the foot, while no part of the artificial covering should be so binding as to prevent the free action of the muscles and the circulation of the blood.

The female shoe or boot now in vogue is, in some respects, very faulty. It has but one good quality, the square or broadly-rounded tip, which is conformable to the natural shape of the end of the foot; and if not made, as it generally is, too tight, would be favorable to the free action so essential to the ease and beauty of the toes. The arch of the shoe is too high, and, pressing strongly upward, weakens and distorts that of the foot.

This defect is increased by an inordinately high and narrow heel, which is, moreover, brought too far forward, with a view of giving an artificial appearance of shortness to the extremity. This position of the heel toward the centre of the foot has the same effect as if the buttress of an architectural arch was removed from the end to its middle. It takes away the strength of its natural prop, and makes it a weakness. It is thus that our dames, in walking, have a hobbling gait, as if their feet were poised upon stilts.

The comfort of the foot is only to be secured by a properly-made shoe, and its beauty preserved by a freedom from unnatural constraint. Where is the modern beauty who would venture to uncover her feet before a royal admirer, as we are told Madame de Pompadour did not hesitate to do? "That which especially astonished the king," says her biographer, "was a pair of pretty bare feet, worthy of marble and the sculptor, in a pair of the most rustic-looking wooden shoes. By a coquetry that was almost artless, the pretty milkmaid (the marchioness was thus disguised) placed one of her feet upon the outside of the wooden shoe. The king recognized the marchioness, and confessed to her that, for the first time in his life, he felt the desire to kiss a pretty foot."

Corns and bunions, those disturbers of human comfort, are not less fatal to grace than to ease. These ugly and painful excrescences are generally produced by an ill-fitting boot or shoe. Too much looseness of the covering of the foot, however, is more apt to beget corns and bunions than excessive tightness. The clumsy, hob-nailed shoe of the plowman, "a mile too big," is oftener a cause than the pinching boot of the exquisite. The corn and bunion, which are produced by friction and irregular pressure, are to be permanently eradicated only by diminishing the one and equalizing the other. The employment of a skillful and judicious shoemaker, who forms his shoes to the feet, and not to the caprice of fashion or of the wearer, will prevent all occasion for consulting the *pedicure*, or foot-doctor. If, however, by any mischance, this best of all preventives fails us, and for our sins we become afflicted with corn or bunion, our only resource is surgical treatment. This is simple, and can be applied by most patients themselves. The excrescence must first be pared down with a sharp knife, and then a piece of amadou, or spunk, as it is familiarly called, with a hole cut in its centre as large as the circumference of the base of the corn, must be thrust over it, and kept in its place by adhesive plaster. This will equalize the pressure of the boot or shoe, and prevent it from rubbing upon the affected part.

The tight shoe or boot, too narrowly toed, is exclusively responsible for that painful affection, *ingrowth* of the toe-nail. If treated in time, it can be easily and simply cured. All that is necessary is to scrape down the nail until it becomes quite thin, and then cut the projecting edge of it in a semilunar form, with its concavity looking outward from the foot. The nail of the great toe should always be thus pared, care being taken not to clip the angles. This causes it to grow toward the centre, and shrink from the tender flesh at the sides.

If the affection has been allowed by neglect to become inveterate, the surgeon must be called in, and he will probably resort to an operation, which, though almost bloodless, is considered one of the most painful of surgery. So painful, indeed, was it known to be, that a famous Parisian surgeon, Velpeau, was in the habit, before the discovery of chloroform, of passing a bandage around the toe, and directing a strong assistant to tighten it with all his might, in order to dull somewhat the sensibility of the part. Chloroform now happily fulfills the blessed service for the rendering of which this awkward process was barely a pretext. Though the operation has thus become painless to the insensible patient, it has lost none of its horror to the spectator. The surgeon, grasping the toe, thrusts the sharp-pointed blade of a pair of scissors under the nail as far as it will go, and then, cutting it in two, tears out each half with a pair of pincers from the quivering flesh in which it has been long imbedded. No one, not even the slave of fashion, should submit to any form of the boot or shoe other than the broad-toed, which is fortunately now in vogue.

The foot, like the hand, is subject to the infirmity of excessive perspiration. It is to be remedied by the same general and local treatment. The habitual daily washing of the feet should be with cold rather than with warm water, and a powder of starch or arrowroot, which it would be well to perfume with bitter almonds, orris, or some other no more intrusive odor, should be sprinkled in the inside of the stocking.

CHAPTER VI.

The Power of Expression and Action.—Freedom and Grace. —A Talleyrand and a Rustic Antinous.—Lord Chesterfield's awkward Man.—Too much Interference.—A wholesome Neglect.—Ugly Tricks of Expression and Gesture. —A wriggling Nose.—The Success of ugly Men.—Submission to the Laws of Nature.—A modern Beauty confronted with the Venus of Milo.—Excessive Fatness and Thinness.—How to be Cured.—Deformities the Result of bad Management in Childhood.—Dancing.—Proper Exercise.—Mind and Body.—Freedom from Restraint.

It is true that regularity of feature and justness of proportion are essential to the perfection of grace. It is, however, no less true that expression, action, and the general carriage of the person have more to do with the figure a man or woman may make in society than any original conformation of body. The laborer stripped to his work in the field may show a form like that of an Antinous, but, placed in the drawing-room by the side of a shriveled, limping Talleyrand, no one would fail to recognize the superior elegance of the cultivated but naturally ill-favored Frenchman. The rustic Antinous, however, if surveyed among his native clods, will probably, as he follows the plow or rests upon his spade, show a natural grace of motion and attitude to which his laced and ruffled victor of the drawing-room could make no pretensions. On his own ground and in the performance of his habitual functions the laborer is at his ease, and each limb and muscle doing its allotted duty fully and freely, his whole well-proportioned frame exhibits all its natural grace. Transferred to the drawing-room, he feels the constraint of strangeness, and with the blankness of clownish amazement upon his face, and stiffness in his joints, the graceful Antinous of the plow becomes an inert monstrosity of human flesh.

There is no more beautiful object in nature than a healthy, well-formed child sporting in the freedom of infancy and innocence. Let it be, however, suddenly placed in the company of strangers, and mark how awe* shadows the face,

* Hogarth, in his *Analysis of Beauty*, notices this effect upon children of the awe produced by the presence of strangers. He says: "It is the cause of their drooping and drawing their chins down into their breasts, and looking under their foreheads as if conscious of their weakness or of something wrong about them. To prevent this awkward shyness, parents and tutors are continually teasing them to hold up their heads, which if they get them to do, it is with difficulty, and, of course, in so constrained a manner that it gives the children pain, so that they naturally take all opportunities of easing themselves by holding down their heads, which posture

and constraint perverts every natural motion of its flexible body to distorted action.

A sense of ease is essential to a graceful carriage of the person, and this is chiefly to be acquired by habitual freedom of motion. All constraint is therefore fatal to it, and none more so than that which comes from the strangeness of a novel position. Grace of bearing in society is almost impossible without frequent association with people of refined manners. "Awkwardness," says Lord Chesterfield, "can proceed but from two causes: either from not having kept good company, or from not having attended to it;" and he shows the effect in this expressive picture: "When an awkward fellow first comes into a room, it is highly probable that his sword

would be full as uneasy to them were it not a relief from restraint; and there is another misfortune in holding down the head, that it is apt to make them bend too much in the back; when this happens to be the case, they then have recourse to steel collars and other iron machines, all which shacklings are repugnant to nature, and may make the body grow crooked. This daily fatigue, both to the children and parents, may be avoided, and an ugly habit prevented, by only (at a proper age) fastening a ribbon to a quantity of plaited hair, or to the cap, so as it may be kept fast in its place, and the other end to the back of the coat, of such a length as may prevent them drawing their chins into their necks; which ribbon will always leave the head at liberty to move in any direction but this awkward one they are apt to fall into."

gets between his legs and throws him down, or makes him stumble, at least. When he has recovered this accident, he goes and places himself in the very place of the whole room where he should not. There he soon lets his hat fall down, and, in taking it up again, throws down his cane; in recovering his cane, his hat falls a second time, so that he is a quarter of an hour before he is in order again. If he drinks tea or coffee, he certainly scalds his mouth, and lets either the cup or the saucer fall, and spills the tea or coffee on his breeches. At dinner his awkwardness distinguishes itself particularly, as he has more to do; there he holds his knife, fork, and spoon differently from other people, eats with his knife, to the great danger of his mouth, picks his teeth with his fork, and puts his spoon, which has been in his throat twenty times, into the dishes again. If he is to carve, he can never hit the joint, but, in his vain efforts to cut through the bone, scatters the sauce in every body's face. He generally daubs himself with soup and grease, though his napkin is commonly stuck through a button-hole and tickles his chin. When he drinks he infallibly coughs in his glass and besprinkles the company. Besides all this, he has strange gestures, such as sniffing up his nose, making faces, putting his fingers in his nose or blowing it, and looking afterward in his handkerchief, so as to make the company sick. His hands are troublesome to him when he has not something in them, and he does not know where to put them, but they are in perpetual motion between his bosom and his breeches. He does not wear his clothes, and, in short, does nothing like other people."

Though it is by the example of good company that the outward graces are chiefly to be acquired, there is undoubtedly something to be learned from precept. Here, however, we would put parents and those who have the control of the young on their guard against the *nimia diligentia*—the too great diligence, or excessive interference with nature, so emphatically denounced by the Roman satirist. The overbusy finger is nowhere more apparent than in the physical rearing of children, who are apt to be regarded merely as lumps of clay, to be fashioned at the will of their parents. They are, however, it should be recollected, living beings, with an inherent principle of growth which is to be developed. The main purpose of education should be to educe this original element, and allow it all the expansion of which it may be capable. It is, however, too often the practice of parents to do the reverse, and try to mould their children into forms of which Nature has given no indication.

The artificial process begins as soon as the child is born. The very swaddling-clothes are so many bonds by which it is restrained of the natural freedom of its body, and its growth so directed that it may assume a shape conformable to some conventional notion or other. This continues from infancy upward, and the dress is a constant obstacle to the natural development of the physical structure. Until the mother gets rid of the idea of *giving* a form to her child, and learns that it is her duty to accept what Nature bestows, the health and vigor of whole generations will continue to be sacrificed. In early youth the great essential of physical development is freedom. The clothes, accordingly, should be so loose as to allow of the freest play of the very flexible body and limbs of infancy and childhood. In the cut of their garments no regard should be had to any fashion or notion of taste which may interfere with ease of movement. It is particularly important that there should be no obstacle in early life to the natural growth, for at that period the human structure is composed of a soft and pliable material, which may be made to assume almost any shape, however perverted; and a deformity thus and then produced will remain a deformity forever.

The over-anxiety of fastidious mothers in regard to the manners of their children leads also to an interference with their grace and vigor of growth. Romping boys and girls are often checked for being noisy, while they should be encouraged. Their racing and shouting are instinctive efforts at development, and essential to the strength of lung and muscle. Those who are unable to bear the noise of children are unfit to have or take charge of them.

The lengthened silence and constrained postures imposed by most school-teachers upon their youthful pupils are as inhuman as they are absurd. Let any grown person, in the possession of all his maturity of strength and power of will, place himself or hold a limb in any fixed position, and see how long he can do either. The action, however easy at first, is soon, if persevered in, followed by weariness and pain. There is only a single posture — that of lying at full length—which can be borne unchanged for a long time. All other positions of the body and limbs being assumed contrary to gravity, and consequently costing an effort of will and muscle, soon become wearisome, and finally impossible. Muscular action requires variety for relief. It is contrary to nature, therefore, for teachers and parents to enforce fixed positions upon their pupils and children. "Hold up your heads!"

"Sit straight!" "Keep down your hands!" "Don't lean on your elbows!" "Don't bend your knees in walking!" and the other importunate commands so often heard in the nursery and school-room, are not seldom harmful interferences with natural action. Nature, after all, is the best posture-master, and gives lessons not only of health, but of genuine grace. Let parents and teachers be less busy, and leave their children's bodies and limbs at least to their natural movements and attitudes. Such an abstinence of interference may appear to careful mothers a neglect, but we assure them that it would be a wholesome neglect.

An awkward carriage or a graceless action, however, may become permanent from carelessness in allowing the young to persist in ugly tricks of attitude, gesture, or expression until they are fixed into habits. There are many of the most offensive practices which can be traced to no other origin than this. We knew an eminent lawyer who had the ugly habit of wriggling his nose in such a manner that, though an orator of unquestionable power, it was difficult to check the disposition to laugh even during his most serious efforts of eloquence, for his unfortunate proboscis seemed always to become excited with the increasing warmth of his rhetoric, and sympathetically to move in quickened action with the hurried flow of his words. This unfortunate nasal wriggle was the result of a trick assumed for diversion in childhood, but so often played that it became a habit too inveterate for control.

Though any great deviations from the average size of the human figure or features do not accord with the general notion of beauty and justness of proportion, it is wiser, as well as more decorous, to submit gracefully, than to make futile attempts to hide or correct them. The shortness of Chesterfield, the fatness of Fox, and the lameness of Talleyrand did not prevent them from shining as exemplars of grace and courtesy. Three of the ugliest men who ever lived, Mirabeau, Wilkes, and Burr, had so far the power of pleasing that few have ever equaled them in gaining the favors of the most beautiful women.

As no one of common decency will refer to the natural infirmity of any person, so the afflicted should make no allusion to it, as is too often done, for they only show, while pretending to indifference, an excessive susceptibility.

Good sense, and, therefore, good taste, for they are inseparably united, dictate submission to the laws of Nature. All interference, consequently, with the natural organization of the body should, as a general rule, be avoided.

Women have been so often and emphatically reminded of the dangers of tight lacing that it is marvelous that they should persist in a practice which they all must know to be at the risk of their lives. Nothing can better show the power of arbitrary Fashion than the subjection of its slaves to this torture of the frame, as fatal to beauty as to health. In reducing the centre of the body to an almost impalpable tenuity, while they laboriously strive, by bulging cotton, crinoline, and outworks of whalebone and wire, to give an unnatural fullness to other parts of the figure to which Nature has refused its fair share of substance, they set at defiance all the laws of proportion. As we stood admiring that most perfect conception of female grace, the Venus of Milo, in the Louvre, we took from the fair woman hanging to our arm her pocket-handkerchief, and made a comparative measurement of the ancient and modern beauties. This was the result: the waist of the statue measured 32 inches in circumference, and the foot 11 inches in length. The waist of the living woman could barely, with all the aid of corset and the various layers of dress, expand to a circumference of 24 inches, while her foot, with shoe and all, was less than 9 inches in length.* With these special diminutions, the modern beauty, however, was by no means generally of dwarfish proportions, and might, within her crinoline and Parisian width of drapery, have enveloped a whole brood of Venuses.

There are certain conditions of the human frame which are due to artificial habits of life. An excessive fatness or meagreness may, for example, be produced by the diet or regimen. In such a case it is obviously not improper to alter them, if thereby the undesirable state of the body can be modified. If over-eating or over-drinking bloats the face and expands unduly the girth, it is undoubtedly right to qualify the strength of the wine and curtail the length of the dinner-courses. People, however, who are constitutionally fat or thin, will find the attempt to shrink or expand themselves seldom successful, and not always safe.

A certain plumpness is essential to the beauty of the female form; but its excess is not considered with us, at least, as an addition to the charms of woman. Africa alone, of all nations—though Turkey has a leaning that way—sets up fatness as a standard of beauty. Cuffey expands female

* These measurements are in proportion to a length of stature of 5 feet 4 inches, which was that of the living person.

loveliness beyond the limits of the embrace of any ordinary mortal, lards it with layers of fat, like a plump partridge prepared for the spit, and feasts his dainty imagination upon the oleaginous charms of female blubber. The Hottentot Venus suckled her young over her shoulder, and carried the rest of her family upon her natural bustle. It is not often that our women, who are generally too nimble in mind and body for its accumulation, complain of fat. Some people, however, have a great tendency to it. This is often hereditary, and shows itself in childhood. There are certain circumstances, moreover, which greatly favor the development of fatness, whether original or acquired. Such are a sedentary life, habits of indulgence, want of light, frequent and prolonged slumber, and physical and moral indolence. A life of wantonness and idleness is said to be the cause of the plumpness of the women of the East, and there is no reason why it should not have the same effect upon those of the West.

The food, however, has more influence than any thing else upon the plumpness of the body, and the effect of quality is greater than that of quantity. Bread, butter, milk, sugar, potatoes, beer, and all spirituous liquors, are particularly fattening. The women of Senegal expand to an extraordinary degree of plenitude, in the course of a few months only, by gorging themselves with fresh dates. Any woman who is troubled with a superfluity of fat, and wishes to get rid of it, can succeed by persevering in a certain diet and regimen. She must live in a warm and dry climate, avoid those articles of diet which are especially fat-producing, and eat those which are not, with a plentiful supply of acids, lead an active life, with brisk exercise both of body and mind, lie on a hard bed, and never remain on it long. To these may be added, with advantage, frequent rubbing of the body with a rough towel or brush, an occasional laxative, alkaline, sea, and vapor baths, with shampooing or kneading of the flesh. Iodine has been occasionally given and found useful. Banting, an Englishman, at the age of sixty-six years reduced himself from two hundred and two pounds (202 lbs.) to one hundred and fifty-six (156 lbs.) in twenty days by the following diet and regimen: For breakfast, 4 or 5 ounces of beef, mutton, kidneys, bacon, or cold meat of any kind, with the exception of fresh pork; a large cup of tea, without sugar or milk, a small biscuit, or an ounce weight of toast. For dinner, 5 or 6 ounces of fish (no salmon) or meat (no fresh pork); all kinds of vegetables except potatoes; an ounce of toast; the fruit, but not the paste of a tart; poultry, game; two or three glasses of good claret, sherry, or Madeira, but no Champagne, port wine, or beer. For tea, 2 or 3 ounces of fruit, about an ounce of toast, and a cup of tea without sugar or milk. For supper, 3 or 4 ounces of such meat or fish as at dinner, with one or two glasses of claret. Before going to bed, if required, a glass of claret or sherry. This plan of Banting has been tried again and again with advantage, and without the least unfavorable accident.

If there are some persons who are anxious to get rid of fat, there are many more, particularly in our country, who are desirous of acquiring it. Thinness is by no means the sign of a bad constitution. On the contrary, it often belongs to the most vigorous of our race. There are, moreover, some charming women, who, though endowed with every other personal attraction, are destitute of that fullness essential to the perfection of the female form. Such, instead of grieving over an organic defect, and resorting to useless and often injurious means to remedy it, should console themselves with their natural fineness of structure, lightness of movement, and the use of such resources as are furnished by a skillful toilet. A regular life, great moderation in pleasure, the avoiding of all social and other dissipation, moderate exercise, light occupation, freedom from nervous excitement, plenty of sleep, and a tranquil and contented spirit, will tend to give flesh to the most meagre. To these must be added a generous diet of meat, vegetables, farinaceous food of all kinds, and a moderate quantity of beer or wine. Fresh milk, taken early in the morning, is said to have a very fattening effect, and frequent warm baths, either simple or emollient, are indispensable.

Dr. Cazenave says that there is nothing more likely to produce excessive thinness than immoderate love, and especially jealousy. Saint Augustine, as quoted by Fénelon, in his treatise on the education of girls, says: "I have seen a baby in arms jealous; it could not pronounce a single word, and already regarded with a pale face and angry eyes another infant who was being suckled at the same time with it." This infantile jealousy is said to be a not uncommon cause of the wasting away of the youngest children. Care, therefore, should be taken to avoid exciting this pernicious passion by a just distribution of care and caress among brothers and sisters.

Ugly deformities are not seldom the result of placing children at the table in chairs of unsuitable height. If the chair is too low, the arms are raised so high as to cause an unsightly elevation of the shoulders, and a consequent sinking, as it were, of the head. Should the chair, on the contrary, be too high, there must be a bending of the neck and upper part of the body, which, if the cause continues long enough, will finally produce a permanent stoop of the shoulders. The chair of the child should be of just the height to bring the elbows, in their natural position, to a level with the table. A too yielding seat, moreover, is bad, as it permits the sinking of the head between the shoulders, and a general drooping of the body. A firm wooden bottom, or, if not easily borne, a carefully stuffed hair cushion should be supplied, and so arranged that it may be raised or depressed to adapt it to the size of the child, or the position of the chair at a table or elsewhere. The lifting or suspension of children by leading-strings is apt to cause that ugliest of deformities, the sinking of the neck between the shoulders.

An ugly gait is often acquired in childhood, which may continue throughout life, by the habit which careless or impatient parents or nurses have of dragging along the little ones they are conducting, and forcing their toddling steps to keep pace with their own striding walk.

In old times dancing was regarded not only as an elegant accomplishment, but as the only means for acquiring the fine and graceful gait suitable for the genteel walks of life. Locke, in his Treatise on Education, says: "Dancing, being that which gives graceful motion to all our limbs, and, above all things, manliness, and a becoming confidence to young children, I think can not be learned too early. Nothing appears to me to give children so much confidence and behavior, and so to raise them to the conversation of those above their years, as dancing."

No one, we suppose, in these liberal days, strenuously opposes dancing if properly regulated, which it seldom is. Our young folks, encouraged by their genteel mammas, cultivate it as diligently as if they thought, with the dancing-master in Molière's comedy, that, though philosophy might possibly be something, there was nothing so necessary to mankind as dancing. It is well, perhaps, that our little masters and misses should subject their flexible feet and limbs to a course of lessons under the fiddle-bow of the dancing-master, and keep themselves in training by an occasional quadrille or waltz. They may thus learn to walk their genteel parts in life with a more assured ease and grace. We can not, however, see the necessity of dancing the German from midnight to four o'clock in the morning, six days out of the seven of each week. On the contrary, it is quite apparent to us that this is an excess which is wholesome neither for body nor mind. It is debauchery, not social enjoyment; and, while it may be favorable to freedom of communion and ease of manners, is conducive neither to a graceful address nor a decorous behavior.

Dancing is a gentle exercise, favorable to the health and graceful development of the body, but, like all physical exercises, must be pursued at seasonable times, and under such circumstances as are dictated by nature, or it will become hurtful. With every additional movement of the limbs the respiration is increased, and the lungs take in a larger supply of air; and this, if not pure, will act upon the system with the virulence of a poison. We need hardly say, what must be obvious to every one who has breathed it, that the atmosphere of the crowded ball-room is not in the condition suitable to health. The apartment is necessarily closed to the severe cold of the winter, and each one of the dense throng which usually gathers at these fashionable dancing-parties is breathing fast under the general agitation of the dance and excitement. The pure air which may have at first existed is sucked up at once, and all, having eagerly consumed the vital element of oxygen it possesses, send it back with the poisonous constituent of carbonic acid gas. The whole room thus soon becomes filled with an atmosphere so vitiated that to breathe the least of it is injurious, and certainly the less of it taken in by the human lungs the better. The dancers, however, by their quickened motion and necessarily increased respiration, are absorbing the most of the poison, while at the same time each one is adding to its virulence. When the air is impure, the greater safety is in repose than in movement. Better no exercise at all than exercise in a poisonous atmosphere, such as must be breathed by our party-going beaux and belles six nights of the week out of the seven.

The exercise of dancing under these circumstances becomes a source, as we all know, of prostration and ill health. No frequenter of the crowded ball will pretend that he or she, after a long night's indulgence in its debaucheries, sleeps more soundly, awakes more refreshingly, and resumes the duties or labors of the day with a lighter step and a livelier spirit. The looks are certainly not improved. Whatever, therefore, may be said in favor of fashionable dancing as a social element, it can not be justified as an exercise favorable to the health or beauty of the body.

The best physical discipline is to be found in

regular and cheerful exercise in the open air. Those sports, which are often termed manly, but are no less womanly, as riding, boating, ball-playing, and brisk walking, are the best means of not only giving strength to the body, but enduing it with grace of form and motion.

Such is the intimate relation between the body and mind that it is impossible to do any good to either unless the actions of both are kept in harmony. This truth is well demonstrated by the utter uselessness of all physical exercise for health's sake, and, we may say, for beauty's sake too, unless accompanied by a wholesome mental activity. Let any one, while depressed in mind, test his muscular power, and he will soon find how little able and disposed he is to use it. On the other hand, if he exerts his physical strength when under the animating influence of pleasurable emotions, he is scarcely conscious of the effort. If physical exercise is persisted in with the indisposition and incapacity for it that come from mental depression, the result is an excessive prostration, which is, of course, injurious to the health of the body. On the contrary, the exertion of the muscular force, stimulated and supported by a cheerful mind, can be continued almost indefinitely, with the good effect of giving increased vigor to the whole human system.

All plans of exercise should be based upon a regard to the harmonious action of mind and body. The solitary "constitutional" walk, as it is called, taken for health's sake, is of no benefit, for it can be seldom varied, and does not supply diversion to the mind, which continues to fret itself and weary the body. Horseback exercise is much superior, for the reason that in the management of the beast there is necessarily a constant call upon the attention which keeps the mental faculties occupied, and thus relieves them of all depressing and exhausting influences.

Those sports requiring physical effort and the open air are excellent for health, as they occupy the mind pleasurably at the same time that they exercise the body. It is surprising how much work can be got out of the muscles when stimulated to action by agreeable emotion. When the mind is cheerful, and thus emancipated from care, the limbs become freer of movement, and of course all the motions and attitudes are more unconstrained and graceful. A child will run, and climb, and tumble, and shout, and indulge in boisterous effort of all kinds the whole day, describing in his vagaries endless lines of beauty, apparently without any fatigue, while engaged in play with his fellows; but let him take the shortest and most composed walk with an elder, and he will hardly step a dozen paces before he begins to lag back in weariness.

The great point to be considered in any plans of exercise for the sake of health and grace is the intimate alliance between body and mind, and the necessity of providing simultaneously for the occupation of both. It matters little how the muscles are put into action; but that form of physical exercise is the best which is accompanied by the most agreeable mental emotions. Pleasant company will give a refreshing, wholesome, and graceful effect to a long walk, which, if taken alone, would only be stiff, wearisome, and weakening.

It is a mistake to suppose that by any kind of fixed physical restraint the human figure can be moulded into beauty, or its movements turned to grace. The surgeon nowadays condemns entirely the bands, stocks, and torturing collars, and boots of iron, with which it was once the custom to strive in vain to bend and twist the youthful twig, and give it a desirable growth of manly or womanly grace. Where there is even a natural deformity, as, for example, in the common bandy leg, it is found that it is more likely to be righted if left to the natural movement and growth of the body than if controlled by artificial means.

The straightness of the trunk of the body of the negro woman of our country and the peasant of Germany has often been noticed, and may be attributed perhaps to the habit common to both of carrying weights upon the head. Where there is a tendency in young girls to a stoop in the shoulders, it may be well to cause them to balance frequently upon their heads a book, or some other object, taking care, however, that it shall not be too heavy, for the excessive loads borne by the German women, though they necessarily give straightness to the back, produce deformity in other parts.

CHAPTER VII.

American Ease.—Propriety of Posture.—A well-bred Person not Demonstrative.—Fuss.—Its Discomforts and Indecorousness.—The Free and Easy.—The Prim.—Fault of the American Walk.—Inelegant Attitudes and Gestures.

WITH all the faults of manner of the American, no one would think of charging him with a want of ease. Generally feeling at home wherever he goes, he is as apt to be "hale fellow well met" with the king on his throne as with the lackey at the palace door. He is not likely to be taken to account for too much stiffness of body and formality of address. His facility of converse and flexibility of limb are proverbial, and few can equal him in expansiveness of sprawl, reach of boot, and readiness of "jaw." He is unapproachable as an acrobat, and his fine chair balance, or trick of heels up and head down, can not be surpassed by any performer on the social stage. When he presents himself, he is not unlike the clown of our early remembrance, who came with a run, a spring, a somersault, and the shout "Here I am!"

We think that many of our countrymen and

countrywomen might be improved by more reserve of manner and less flexibility of limb. Americans can dispense with much freedom of movement and looseness of posture, as indeed of ease of address, without any risk of incurring the imputation of being prigs. In society ordinarily termed good, it is not customary to sit upon more than one chair at a time, nor is the mantelpiece regarded as the proper place for the feet, however well turned the boot or delicately made the shoe. Sprawling of all kinds is avoided by well-bred people, who shun excessive ease as much as excessive formality. It may not be amiss to remind the heedless and the young that, on entering the room of the house of a stranger or that of a visiting acquaintance, it is not becoming to throw themselves at once on the sofa and stretch out their legs, or into the Voltaire or easy-chair, and sink into its luxurious depths. The common seat will be selected by the considerate, and all the exceptional provisions for extra ease and comfort left untouched until the invitation to enjoy them is given.

A well-bred person is ordinarily disinclined to make a public demonstration of his most affectionate feelings and tenderest sentiments. He therefore rarely kisses, weeps, embraces, or sighs before strangers or formal acquaintances. Fuss is, above all things, his horror, and he strives to check every noisy or uneasy indication of emotion and passion.

It has always been considered by the best-bred people that fuss of any kind was inconsistent with good manners. The English aristocracy, however unworthy of imitation in some respects many may deem them, are universally regarded as safe examples to follow in all matters of ceremonious behavior. Well, there is nothing a "My Lord" or "My Lady" so studiously avoids as fuss.

Quietness in all things is an essential element of a well-bred English person. He shuns all outward display of his personality. He cares not to be seen or heard, and rests content with being felt as a power in the land. He thus not only eschews noisy and grandiloquent talk, but all showy and noticeable costume. His voice is low, his words simple, his action grave, and his dress plain. He holds himself so habitually under constraint that his nerves never seem to vibrate with emotion. He becomes, as it were, an impassible being, upon whom no external cause seems capable of making an impression.

We do not wish to hold up the Lord Dundrearys as models to our republican citizens to mould themselves by. The unemotional Englishman, in his excess of impassibility, is a cold, unfeeling person, and only interesting as a humorous exaggeration in a farce. We do not desire that our red-hot enthusiasts should be cooled down to the extreme degree of that frigid John Bull who could look into the crater of Mount Vesuvius and see "nothing in it," or quietly scan with his glass a drowning fellow-mortal, and refuse to lend him a helping hand because he had never been introduced to him. There is a wide range of the moral thermometer between the zero of English frigidity and the usual high degree of American ebullition.

There is this obvious advantage in habitually checking the tendency to excitement, that we acquire such a control over our emotions that, in cases of emergency, our reason is left free to act. The film of feeling is removed from the eye, and the nature of the danger is clearly discerned. An excited person is always moving in a fog, and he may at any time plunge into a quagmire or fall headlong down a precipice.

Fuss is a great obstacle to comfort. Its effect is not only to heighten the unavoidable miseries of life, but to create unnecessary ones. Its influence is chiefly apparent in the small annoyances of daily existence. The heavy strokes of fate fall with such a crushing force upon the

sensibility that it becomes at once too prostrate to be capable of fuss. Grief subdues and makes silent, but vexation excites and creates noise.

It is astonishing how much misery—small, perhaps, in detail, but immense in the aggregate—is voluntarily imposed upon self and others by fussy people. Take, for example, the grossly exaggerated if not entirely simulated maladies which the fashionable doctors tell us form two thirds of their cases. What a fuss is made by the pretended victims! and who can measure the degree of real suffering they inflict upon others? How often are whole families, and even communities, made miserable by these chronic complainers, who not seldom survive long enough to worry out of existence several generations by unnecessary fuss!

Fuss is vulgarly supposed to be essential to a good housekeeper. It is not really so, for quiet is as necessary to excellence of housewifery as smoothness of work to goodness of machinery. It is quite a mistake to suppose that the unavoidable misery of "washing day" is more effectually got over by fussing about it the whole week before and after. It is no less so to imagine that the necessary evil of house-cleaning, or pickling, or any other domestic trial of periodical occurrence, is to be endured more patiently

by twelve months of daily anticipatory fussing. We doubt, moreover, whether we get a perfect and agreeable idea of cleanliness when constantly reminded, by the ever-present wet clouts, scrubbing-brushes, soap-suds, bare floors, and uncarpeted staircases, of the ceaseless efforts of a fussy housekeeper.

There is nothing more fatal to comfort as well as to decorum of behavior than Fuss.

The excessive flexibility of limb which distinguishes the American shows itself in the free use of his hands and arms, as well as legs and feet. He no sooner finds himself in the presence of a stranger than he coils his arms about his body and squeezes him into an appreciation of the warmth of his friendship, or awakens him by a sharp slap upon the back into a sudden consciousness of its strength. "Hands off!" may be seen by a discerning person, as clearly as if the words were printed, to be posted all over well-bred people. There is nothing a fastidious person dislikes so much as the careless or intentional touch of the stranger. It behooves every one, therefore, to keep his eyes open, that he may read this warning, and recollect that he has no right of common in the shoulders of every fellow-mortal he meets, however broad and easy of approach they may be.

Of course it is not to be inferred that, though the "free and easy" may be the characteristic defect of the manners of most Americans, there are not some to be found whose prevailing fault is the reverse of an unconstrained ease. There are occasional persons to be seen, especially in the eastern parts of our broad territory, whose practice, at any rate, if not theory, is by no means in the direction of Hogarth's wavy line of beauty. These good people of genuine Puritan descent have somehow or other confounded morals with physics, and seemingly regard it as wicked to diverge from the line of the perpendicular as from religious rectitude. Primness of manners is by no means graceful, and we would remind our young folks that their bodies are so constructed anatomically as to be capable of bending without breaking. In bowing or courtesying they will find it by no means fatal to their own gravitation and resistance to yield to the natural elasticity of their frames, though, if they refuse to do so, it may be trying to other people's gravity and self-command.

Many dames, by not bending the knees, render their walk very ungraceful. The posture, moreover, if too rigid, particularly in sitting, has an exceedingly ugly look. Some folks are unable to sit on a chair, though they have so many opportunities of learning how to do it. While some never fairly get on a seat but to their own manifest discomfort and that of all who look upon their misery poise and balance themselves on the sharp edge, there are others who roll their bodies up into heaps, as it were, and throw them with an audible bounce deep into the receptacle, whatever it may be. Every one seating himself should take his place deliberately, and so completely that he may feel the full repose of the chair, which it is designed to give. The limbs, once at rest, should be moved, if moved at all, as noiselessly as possible; and all extraordinary actions, such as lifting, for example, one leg high upon the other, and holding it there manacled by a grasp of the hand, should be avoided. A person striding a chair, and grinding his teeth, and thrumming his hands on the back, has by no means an elegant look to the observer before or behind. This practice, which is never becoming in any company, is simply indecent in that of women.

CHAPTER VIII.

The Expression.—How far Involuntary.—Laughter.—Its Propriety.—Its Advantages.—Blushing.—Shamefacedness.—Hawthorne in Company.—Great Men, Men of Society.—The Disguises of Age.—Too much Hair.—Hair-dressing.—Misuse of the Nose.—Artificial Odors.

THE face may manifest, more or less independently of the will, the character of the person, yet it can be made, by set purpose, to assume an expression by no means indicative of the predominating moral or intellectual quality. Thus there are some countenances, as those of the hypocritical, which, by studied care and long practice, are made to give signs directly the reverse of the true character. There are others, again, in which the expression is so designedly obscured that it may be totally unreadable. These are the inscrutable faces which are not seldom found among consummate thieves and their skillful catchers and detectives.

The expression is undoubtedly greatly under the control which every polite person is constantly exercising. It often occurs that we are provoked to a manifestation of emotion the reverse of what is proper to the occasion. The provocative is of course resisted, and generally with success, by the decorous. No decent person laughs at a funeral or weeps at a wedding, although the disposition is not seldom strongly felt to reverse the conventional order of the tear and the smile.

It would seem that polite persons are expected to cultivate a uniform composure of face. Lord Chesterfield says, "I am sure that, since I have had the full use of my reason, nobody has ever heard me laugh," and denounces "frequent and loud laughter as the characteristic of folly and of ill manners." So far his lordship may be right, and we agree with him when he adds that people of sense and breeding should be above laughing at buffoonery or silly accidents; but we protest against his broad assertion that "there is nothing so illiberal and so ill bred as audible laughter," and that "true wit or sense never yet made any body laugh; they are above it; they please the mind, and give a cheerfulness to the countenance."

Laughing inappropriately and on all occasions is certainly an offensive habit. This is partly attributed by Chesterfield to awkwardness and *mauvaise honte*, and he gives as an example the case of a famous poet. "I know a man," says he, "of very good parts, Mr. Waller, who can not say the commonest thing without laughing, which makes those who do not know him take him at first sight for a natural fool."

Much can be said in favor of laughter. Socially it has the inspiriting influence of Champagne, promoting general gayety. Of course, opportunity and a decorous moderation should regulate the indulgence in this, as in all other pleasures; but we protest against the total banishment of hearty laughter from polite society. Its good effects upon the individual, as well as upon mankind in the aggregate, can not be spared. Without it, the national character would wither to a dryness in which there would be no succulence of humor, physical or moral, left.

Laughter, which is the ordinary physical manifestation of the sentiment of mirth, is peculiarly favorable to health. Its action, starting with the lungs, diaphragm, and contiguous muscles, is conveyed to the whole body, "shaking the sides," and producing that general jelly-like vibration of which we are so agreeably conscious when under its influence. This wholesome exercise is, moreover, preceded and accompanied by a gently exciting emotion of the mind, than which nothing can be more favorable to the health. The human being thus receives, mentally and bodily, an impulse which gives renewed force to every vital organ. The heart beats more briskly, and sends its life-giving fluid to the smallest and most distant vessel. The face glows with warmth and color, the eye brightens, and the whole temperature of the body is heightened. When laughter and the emotions which provoke it become habitual, the effect is to increase the insensible perspiration of the skin, to quicken breathing, and expand the lungs and chest, to strengthen the power of digestion, and favor nutrition. The proverb "Laugh and grow fat" states a scientific truth. Shakspeare recognizes the influence of mirth upon the human body in his description of the "spare Cassius:"

"Seldom he smiles."

It is a well-known fact that joy and its manifestations are the best sharpeners of the appetite. Dyspepsia has been truly said to commence oftener in the brain than in the stomach, being so generally produced by anxiety of mind and want of cheerfulness. A social feast, with its accompaniments of jollity and good-fellowship, is less apt to disorder a delicate digestion than the solitary anchorite's crust and cress.

The agreeable emotions are the most effective preventives of disease. During the prevalence of epidemics the courageous and cheerful are seldom attacked. The plague, it has been said, is a magnanimous enemy, and spares the brave. Those who give way to the depressing emotions, such as fear and anxiety, are, on the contrary, the first victims. There is an Eastern apologue which describes a stranger on the road meeting the Plague coming out of Bagdad. "You have been committing great havoc there," said the traveler, pointing to the city. "Not so great!" replied the Plague. "I only killed one third of those who died; the other two thirds killed themselves with fright." The doctors tell us that a man may be daily exposed for weeks or months, perhaps for years, to marsh miasms or malaria, to the contagion of the most malignant diseases—typhus fever, scarlatina, or cholera—with impunity, provided he keeps up a merry heart. The Walcheren pestilence, which proved finally so destructive to the British troops, never tainted a soldier with its fatal touch until the expedition became manifestly a failure. While cheered by the hope of victory, each bid defiance to disease; when depressed with certainty of defeat, every one became a ready victim.

Cheerfulness is not only an effective preventive of disease, but an excellent remedy. Nothing is observed to be so unfavorable to the return to health of a sick man as despair of himself, while hopefulness of his own case acts as the most potent restorative.

Lord Bacon says: "To be free-minded and cheerfully-disposed at hours of meat, and sleep, and of exercise, is one of the best precepts of long lasting." It may be doubted whether a lugubrious man ever fulfilled the allotted period of threescore years and ten, while it is notorious that all those who have greatly surpassed it have been mirthful persons.

The celebrated Sydenham was so persuaded of the efficacy of cheerful emotions in the treatment of disease, that he was accustomed to recommend to his patients the perusal of "Don Quixote," saying, "If you want to get well, read that and laugh."

Blushing, which, as a sign of modesty, may be commendable in the young, especially of the female sex, is by no means always pleasing and worthy of encouragement. When immoderate and inopportune, it becomes a social nuisance. There is a false shame, or *mauvaise honte*, as the French call it, which is the very reverse of true modesty. The usual signs of the fictitious quality are shyness, with the common accompaniments of frequent and ill-timed blushing, hesitancy of speech, hanging of the head, downcast eyes, sidelong glances, shambling and stumbling gait, restlessness of posture, and a general air of voluntary shrinkage, if we may be allowed the term. This false modesty is the result of a genuine vanity, which, overestimating self, fancies it the object of universal attention. This naturally begets a sensitiveness and an anxiety about personal appearance so great that they embarrass the whole behavior; for these excessively vain persons, fancying all eyes constantly upon them, would desire to make a figure in society of which they are manifestly incapable. Of this they are the first to become conscious, and their hopelessness of success is painted in strong colors upon the face, and visibly impressed upon every limb and feature. There are persons who live to an advanced life, and yet retain this *mauvaise honte.* It has often proved fatal to the social qualities of some who have been otherwise singularly well adapted not only to receive from society, but to bestow upon it, both distinction and happiness. Hawthorne, our American genius, of whom we are justly proud, was so afflicted with this *mauvaise honte* that, with a head like that of Jove, and a natural majesty that might have become the throne of Olympus, would shrink, blush, hang his head, and hesitate in speech before a stranger, like an awkward school-boy. In his case, it is true, if there was self-consciousness of importance, it was greatly justified, but it is no less true that its excessive manifestation made him entirely impracticable as a member of general society, which was undoubtedly the chief loser in this instance, though ordinarily it is not. If men of genius, like Lafontaine, Cowper, and Hawthorne, may be allowed to turn their heads and fly from the ordinary world, it is not permissible for the every-day people of whom society is generally composed to shirk the duties such a brotherhood imposes. All young men and women should be held amenable to the obligations of social decorum; and, in case of neglect or disobedience, nothing less than genius, and that not without a thorough sifting of the claim, should be received in extenuation. It is not to be inferred that great endowments of intellect are necessarily or even commonly associated with a deficiency of social qualities. Shakspeare, Bacon, Newton, Franklin, and Scott were men of society. All, indeed, were public personages, and called upon to fulfill duties which any false modesty would have rendered impracticable.

The art of "growing old gracefully" is shown in no respect more evidently than by the discretion with which the marks of age are treated. No devices to give a deceitful appearance of youth can be justified by the sense of fitness and good taste. False hair, more particularly, is among the ugliest of shams, and, though made temporarily current by the sanction of fashion, can not withstand the test of a severe decorum. Old people of the best breeding now seldom resort to the hair-dresser to refurbish their shattered and decaying frames. The wig and dye-pot are, we are pleased to announce, going out of fashion.

The hair of the young, according to our taste, should indicate as little as possible the artificial touch of the *coiffeur*. At any rate, any marked evidence of his fanciful, oily, and odorous fingers is always disgusting. When once the head has been properly arranged, it is well to avoid all farther interference with it. The practice, so common with men, of passing the hands through the locks, and of women of titivating them with their gentle touches, is filthy, and not becoming before company. The use of a comb, or even its habitual carriage in the pocket, is irreconcilable with all nicety of manners. Some otherwise very decent people, however, have this vile practice, and it is not uncommon to find them deliberately combing themselves at the table common to many guests.

The nose is the most prominent and noticeable

feature of the face, and, as its functions are not all of the noblest kind, it especially behooves people who desire to be nice to avoid drawing attention to them. Consequently, all its requirements should be attended to in the quietest and most private manner possible. It should never be fondled before company, or, in fact, touched at any time, unless absolutely necessary. The nose, like all other organs, augments in size by frequent handling, so we recommend every person to keep his own fingers, as well as those of his friends or enemies, away from it.

We need hardly protest against the misuse of the nose in turning it into a dust-hole or a soot-bag, for the habit of snuff-taking has gone so out of fashion that we can hardly find now even a grandmother to venture upon a pinch. This habit, apart from its filthiness, weakens the senses of smell and hearing, and perverts the human voice to a grunt by thickening the soft and sensitive membrane which extends without a break through the nose, ear, and throat, every part of which is reached by the irritating particles of the tobacco inhaled.

Most nations, not content with the sweet odors* that Nature so bountifully supplies, re-

* The labor and cost which man will endure for the small luxury of a smell are exemplified by the difficulty and ex-

H

sort to artificial sources. The most refined people, however, avoid as much as possible personal perfumes, and hold that the absence of all odor is the best savor of human communion. They agree with Lord Bacon that the "breath of flowers is far sweeter in the air, where it comes and goes, like the warbling of music, than in the hand." Those of nice taste eschew all perfumes but those which are evanescent, such as Cologne and the like. It is a curious fact that the *eau de Cologne* is a native of that worst smelling of cities where Coleridge smelt we forget how many stenches. This seems to confirm the suspicion that a perfume is but a mask for an ill odor. The Cologne owes its well-deserved reputation to the harmonious mixture of a variety of essences, chiefly those of lemon, juniper, and rosemary, so well combined that there is no predominating smell. It is, moreover, very evanescent, and has a spirituous and enlivening scent, which causes it to be used rather for one's own refreshment than for the delectation of others. This should be the rule in regard to all perfumes.

pense of manufacturing the attar or otto of roses. Two grains only, it is said, of oil can be squeezed with the utmost care from a thousand roses, and this is sold in India, on the spot where it is made, for fifty dollars in gold a rupee in weight, which is about 176 grains. At two grains a thousand, a rupee of oil would require nearly ninety thousand roses!

They should be kept as far as possible for the individual, and never employed so strong as to penetrate the surrounding atmosphere. All intensely adherent smells, such as musk, should be carefully eschewed.

CHAPTER IX.

Discreet Use of the Eye.—Familiar Glances.—The Fashion of Eye-glasses.—Fast Girls.—Winking.—Sleeping in Company.—The Somnolence of Washington Irving.—Ear-boring.—Its Cruelty and Barbarism.

As the eye is the most expressive feature of the face, so is it the one above all which should be used with particular discretion. The two extremes of shyness and boldness, as indicated by the downcast look and the staring, are equally unbecoming. During ordinary social intercourse with an equal, the eyes should be raised to his or hers with a regard neither very unsteady nor fixed. The look must not be staring or scrutinizing, but mildly inquiring and sympathetic.

We doubt whether the free interchange of glance between those of opposite sex, so common even among the pretenders to good breeding, can be justified by the principles of true decorum. There is to be noticed in the public promenades, the ballrooms, the operas, the theatres, and even in the churches, a wondrous familiarity of look between our beaux and belles, who, though strangers to each other, thus seem to have established, in the twinkle of an eye, an intimacy of intercourse they would never acknowledge.

The free eye is a marked characteristic of the libertine, and all modest women should turn persistently from its roving and unlicensed glances. Some young girls of the *fast* kind, with an audacious defiance of conventional propriety, and yet often with no thought of offense against real modesty, will not only recklessly dally with these intrusive looks, but not seldom venture a cast of them on their own account.

There are fast women every where, but the fast girl seems to be more particularly an American product. A tendency on the part of the young, unmarried female to eccentric flights of any kind is effectually checked in most countries by parental control. This continues to assert itself vigorously until marriage. A young girl in Europe, except in England, where the social customs are more like our own, has thus little opportunity of indulging in fastness or any other maiden vagary.

The unmarried American woman is discerned at once by the freedom of her manners. Her bearing, of course, is modified more or less by the natural disposition, education, and surrounding influences; but there is always apparent, even in the most reserved, that sense of independence characteristic of the republican maid. You see at once, in the face of the most modest, the well-assured look of the conscious will.

Without the least disposition to fasten European social fetters upon our daughters of Freedom, we would remind them that there are certain laws of taste and propriety as obligatory on their obedience as upon that of their sisters of monarchical England or imperial France. Liberty is not necessarily license, and the claim to the one is not to be vindicated by the lawlessness of the other. The American girl is no more free by right than any other to indulge in those bold coquetries with indecorum, whether of dress, conversation, or manners, comprehended within the slang term of fastness. It is, moreover, a paltry ambition, and not without risk to virtue, to aspire to the distinction of being pointed out as "the low-necked" Bel Smith, or the "high-stepping" Fanny Jones, or the girl who drank a whole bottle of Champagne, or she who smoked one of Frank Tripup's fifty-cent regalias. These, or the improprieties they may symbolize, are too common to be considered any longer eccentricities. They are indeed fast becoming such prevalent characteristics as to mark the type of the young girl of fashion. Her essential defect is a vulgar ambition for notoriety. She will endure any thing but obscurity, and therefore takes care that she is seen, heard, and talked of by all the world. Her dress is accordingly flaunting, her voice loud, her words slangy, her eye staring, her manners obtrusive, and conduct audaciously irregular. All this may be, and is, doubtless, done without any overt act of vice, but it looks so much like it that the difference is hardly perceptible to the external observer. In fact, it seems to be the purpose of the fast damsel to assume the semblance of wickedness, for in this exhausted age the piquancy of sin is essential to awaken admiration; and hypocrisy, ceasing to pay its tribute to virtue, pays it to vice. The danger of this is obvious, for familiarity with the forms is apt to endanger indifference to the substance. The effect upon manners and character, even when the last and fatal step is not taken, is exceedingly hurtful. The young maid, in droping her reserve, loses her distinctive charm, and the steady eye and defiant forehead alarm those to whom the look of modesty is so alluring. The bold and flaunting girl can never become the orderly housewife and patient mother, for will she be contented to perform the quiet duties of home, and accept the secret approval of her own conscience, after having been accustomed to public display and notoriety?

It would seem that American parents might curtail somewhat the liberty of their children, without interfering too much with that independence of action so essential to the strength of character. Girls are allowed to consider themselves women too soon, and are thus prematurely emancipated from parental control. They are, moreover, after leaving school, permitted to remain mistresses of their own time, when they should be held in subjection to a systematic discipline of study and conduct. With less idle time and a more watchful parental care, there would be fewer of those fast girls, whose eccentricities are becoming daily more remarkable and alarming, and who are destined, if not checked in their growth, to have a disastrous effect upon social manners and morals.

After this long digression, into which we have been led by the convenience of the occasion and the importance of what we had to say, we return to our subject. The functions of the natural eye and eye-glasses are much abused. It is quite clear that the whole world of fashion has not all of a sudden become so afflicted with shortsightedness as to render the use of artificial means for its relief universally necessary. Nine tenths of the people, male and female, who are constantly eying the universe and each other through glass, require no other medium than the one provided by Nature. Nothing can be more ill bred, and we assert it in the face of assenting Fashion, than ogling a stranger in the streets through an eye-glass—

"With a stony British stare,"

or surveying an opposite neighbor at the theatre with a lorgnette.

We were witnesses of a deserved rebuke gently given by a priest at *Notre Dame*, in Paris, to a young American girl who, during matins, was freely using her eye-glass. He touched her arm, and indicated her wrong-doing with a frown so polite that it might almost be taken for a smile. She received the chiding with a graciousness which nearly atoned for her sacrilegious offense, and the fair penitent will, we are sure, sin no more in this respect, wherever she may go.

Winking and all knowing glances had better be left to the horse-jockeys and the frequenters of the bar-rooms, billiard saloon, and gambling-tables. It would seem hardly necessary to remind any one of the indecorousness of sleeping in company, but it must be recollected that the obligation is equally urgent upon all not to put people to sleep. It is the duty of every one to be wakeful; it is equally so to be as little somniferous in matter and manner as possible. An illustration is given in Vivian Gray of the somnolency of Washington Irving, who, according to the author, D'Israeli, was taken up bodily from a dinner-table where he had fallen asleep, and did not awake until set down in the midst of an evening party. This, if true, should be put down rather to the account of the stupidity of London dinners than the impoliteness of Irving, who, of all men, was the most courteous.

The ear is naturally one of the most retiring features of the face, and therefore less often offends than is offended against. We may suggest, however, the propriety of restricting to the private dressing-room all that is necessary for its toilette, as well as that of the rest of the person. The insertion of the finger or any instrument into the passages of the ear, however necessary for keeping that important organ in proper order, is entirely an operation of private, and not public interest.

We must here, even at the risk of a universal oh! from all womankind, protest against the barbaric practice of ear-boring, to which they cling with a singular persistence. It would be as difficult, probably, to dissuade our dames from making holes in their ears and hanging trinkets to them as it would be to induce a female Hottentot to forego the national fashion of piercing the cartilage of her flattened nose and suspending from it a ring, large and heavy as an iron cable-link, or prevent a Feejee Islander from tearing with a jagged fish-bone a rent in the nether lip big and ugly as her voracious mouth. The practice, however, of so-called civilized women is no less barbaric than that of these savage females.

The woman of ancient Greece, true to the instinctive sense of beauty and cultivated grace of her race, trusted to the developments of her natural charms for attractive force, and scorned all adornments which were not inherent in her own person. Fancy those beautiful ear-pulps of the Venus of Milo, just peeping from below her wavy garland of hair, bored through and through, and dragged out from their cozy shelter by heavy pendants of gold, silver, or what not. Who would not be struck aghast at such a sacrilege of art and nature?

More modern art accepted these barbaric baubles. Titian, for example, puts them in the ears of his Venus, but in the voluptuousness of that conception how great is the change, we might say degradation, from the God-like chasteness of the Greek ideals of beauty!

So fixed is the attachment of modern women

to this ugly and barbaric practice, that they not only persist themselves in wearing ear-rings, but enjoin it almost as a duty upon their daughters to do likewise. No sooner has the offspring of fashion, Miss Arabella Augusta, or plain Maggie of the common world—for the habit is universal—completed her first decade, than she is taken to some jeweler or surgeon (for there are even surgeons found thus to degrade their noble art) to have her ears *bored.* The little ones seldom go unwillingly, so early are they disposed to offer themselves as sacrifices to that exacting deity, Fashion. In fact, we know of one impatient little hussy who, unwilling to bide her mother's time, actually dropped the stocking she was darning, and with the great needle deliberately pierced holes in her ears, and left in each a string of yarn to fester and complete the mutilation.

The ordinary process of ear-boring is simple, and seldom either very painful or dangerous, although there are cases recorded of erysipelas and death having followed. The operator, be he jeweler or surgeon, holds a cork firmly against one side of the lobe of the ear, while from the other side he transfixes it with a needle or an awl, as a saddler punches a hole into a leather strap. Then a thread is passed through and left to fester, so that the opening once made may not close again. Familiar as you are with the process, for it is being performed in each day's light of this civilized land, gentle and Christian dames, does not this description of it, when deliberately read, sound like that of the barbarous practice of savages in some far-off country of heathenism?

By hazard we once saw a young girl thus mutilated. She came into a jeweler's shop clinging to a great blowzy woman bejeweled all over from the lobes of her ears to the tips of her fingers, and her toes too, for what we know. The child was pale, but was biting her lower lip with a spasmodic fixedness of resolution. The operator, a great whiskered fellow, after fumbling about for his tools, finally brought out his awl and cork and began the operation. With the mere touch of the cutting instrument the poor child winced for the first time, and as the man, who was somewhat of a bungler, forced his way, boring through the tender flesh, a tear was wrung from each little eye, and drop after drop of blood fell and splashed, making great red stains upon her linen collar. The child only bit her lip more firmly, but evidently could hardly restrain herself, and would have cried if her vanity had allowed. The operator coolly wiped his bloody instrument, and the mother warmly scolded the child for letting the blood drop upon her collar, and, paying the price of her child's mutilation, walked away, still grumbling at the stains.

Mothers will sometimes, when pressed hard to answer for this barbarity, declare that boring the ears is good for the eyes. This is a vulgar error, and only worthy of a greasy ship's cook or ignorant Maltese sailor, who wears ear-rings, as he says, for the same reason.

Neither is there beauty or fitness in the practice of hanging the ears with trinkets. The ear was intended to lie half concealed by the hair, and any thing attached to it brings it into undue prominence. The ear-ring, however precious and pretty in itself, does not add beauty to that rarest of possessions, a small and well-formed ear, while it draws attention to a big oyster-like one, and intensifies its ugliness.

CHAPTER X.

Purity of Speech.—Effect of refined Association.—Exaggeration of American Talk.—Fashionable Falsehood.—Plain Speaking.—Prudishness of Speech.

Good early culture and habitual association with refined persons are undoubtedly essential to give purity to speech and the highest tone of refinement to conversation. There are many persons who have diligently perfected themselves in a knowledge of the laws of grammar, and become familiar with the style of the chastest writers, and yet can not utter a phrase without betraying the barbarism of a rude origin. It is not uncommon to find people learned in all the rules of syntax, and capable of applying them to the art of writing, who habitually speak incorrectly. Those, too, who are precisians in speech are often ignorant of, and unrestrained by, the laws of grammar in writing. A correct and refined pronunciation, especially, is only to be acquired by hearing it constantly, and from the earliest age, from the lips of those who habitually use it. It is said that Sir Robert Peel, the great English statesman, with all the refinements of his school, collegiate, and social relations, was never thoroughly able to overcome the early influence of his humble Lancashire origin, and that, during all his life, the *h* was to him, as to most of his countrymen, a constant stumbling-block.

It would be presumptuous to pretend to give precepts for the acquisition of a refined speech, which is only to be obtained by personal communion with the expert. It is well, however, to suggest the importance of keeping the young, as far as possible, within the sound of pure speaking, and not trust to the schoolmaster and the rules of grammar for perfecting them in the refinements of speech. The choice of servants becomes important in this regard, and we doubt whether the rude peasants of the Black Forest and bogs of Connemara, to whom we commonly intrust our little ones, are better suited to give sweetness of voice, justness of emphasis, and correctness of expression than refinement of manners to the future cavaliers and dames of America.

Although we can not pretend to give perfection to the use of mouth and tongue by any thing we may say, we shall venture to utter a few warnings, with the hope of preventing the abuse of those flexible and easily perverted organs.

Loudness, or what the French call the *criard*,

is peculiarly an attribute of American talk, and is not favorable to purity of diction or clearness of thought. This style of conversation is marked by the free use of intense and high-sounding adjectives, generally employed in their superlative degrees. These, moreover, are often most ludicrously misapplied. For example, we hear the "splendidest" weather, the "most beautiful" ice-cream, the "sweetest" clergyman, the "most elegant" sermon, the "awfulest" fine whiskers, the "terrible dress that horrid Miss A—— wore," the "dreadfully shocking" hat of Miss B——, and those "magnificent" trowsers of Harry, and "delicious" boots of Tom, gushing from the lips of our young damsels in a torrent of such confused speech that its parts are hardly distinguishable from each other, and form but a turbid mixture of nonsense.

Every few years or so a slang phrase gets somehow or other into vogue. That this should consist merely of the misuse of some familiar term, and not the invention of a new one, like "quiz," for example, shows the comparative poverty of device of us moderns. "Awful" is, for the moment, the abused word, and it is bandied about throughout all the length and breadth of the English language, and consequently all over the globe. For no reason in the world, it has thrown out of usage an appropriate and serviceable adverb, and suddenly taken its place, for which, being an adjective, it is by nature unfit. Wherever the old "very" once becomingly held its own, the impudent interloper "awful" has thrust itself, contrary to all grammatical decorum. Slang of every variety, whether consisting of this absurd abuse of a word, or whatever else, is equally opposed to correctness of speech and propriety of manners.

Profane swearing, or its relatives, the various emphatic expletives, are now never heard in decent society, and people of good breeding are not expected to give pledges of "word" or "honor" as guarantees of their truth and honesty.

There is a kind of deceit which fashion seems to sanction, but the necessity or convenience of which may not be so great as is supposed. It is astonishing the number of falsehoods one has to utter to make a respectable figure in what is technically called society. A truthful person, incapable of practicing a deceit or asserting a lie, would not be able to hold up her head for a moment in what the fashionable deem good company. Fancy a woman with a conscience above deception presenting herself in all her naturalness of person and character! Suppose her, scorning crinoline, padding, false hair, and other artifices of the modern dame's *make-up*, and exhibiting herself in her original dimensions! Nothing would so shock the sensibilities of the fashionable world at least as such an honest disclosure of the truth—of nature.

The proprieties of society would be still further startled at the sound of the spoken truth. If any one should drop the lying words of love, friendship, esteem, and admiration, and use only those expressions which denote the actual relations of ordinary mortals, he or she would be speedily thrust out.

We are told that these expressions of endearment and of proffered service so universal are merely conventional expressions; that, for example, when we say or write to persons the most indifferent to us, as we all do, "My dear Sir," or "Dear Madam," "Your humble servant," or "Yours faithfully," we do not mean what is said or written. We are quite aware of it, and this only confirms our statement of the social necessity of the lie; for in the most ordinary relations of life we are compelled to make use of it, or lose our claim to a place in polite society. Some ingenious moralists have found excuses for the conventional falsehood. We are rejoiced that they have, for it seems impossible to avoid telling it; and many a sore conscience wants salving. Paley justifies a dame, who *is* at home, saying that she is *not*, by the gloss that she means that "she is not at home to see company." This is no justification at all; for if she does not desire to deceive, why should she not state the plain truth.

While allowing largely for the quantity of falsehood necessary to make a respectable appearance in society, we still think that there is an exorbitant use of that tempting but fatal vice. The great danger of conceding the least privilege to a lie is that it may assert its right of way every where; and it is a fact that where the conventional falsehood is most in vogue, there genuine truth is least common. It is astonishing with what effrontery a fashionable woman will tell a barefaced lie! Mark with what rapidity she will pass from a compliment to abuse of the same person! She is "charmed" and "disgusted" in the turn of a heel; praises before and vituperates behind; welcomes loudly in a voice which ends in a whisper of discontent; and one half of her time is spent in unsaying what she says during the other. A dame of "the best society" urged, in our hearing, with apparent candor and earnestness, a gentle guest to favor the company with the pleasure of hearing her "sweet voice." The young girl no sooner turned with a polite compliance to the piano than our hostess whispered to another guest at her side, "Now you'll hear a screech." The compliment and denunciation were uttered almost in the same breath, and without a change in the uniform ripple of her face.

How many urgent solicitations are made to which the "favorable" answer desired is a negative, though the contrary is pretended with so much apparent earnestness. When people are asked to "stay," to "call again," to "come often," to "drop in to dinner," "to be sure to be in time for tea," it is seldom wished they should do either. These are the polite lies and frauds of society which can not be justified by any abstract principle of morals.

There is a habit the directly opposite of fashionable falsehood; we mean plain speaking, of which we shall find no traces in polite society. This, though undoubtedly a virtue, may be carried to an uncomfortable and inconvenient excess.

There are certain people who take credit to themselves for seeing through all the illusions of life, and tearing away every veil of gauze which individual fondness or social propriety may throw over the ugly and painful. These run a muck through society, attacking all its cherished deceits, however innocent and harmless. They would make a clean sweep of all the phantasms of the imagination, put to flight the airy creations of the fancy, and dispel the cloudless visions of dreamland. They would not that man should ever forget his primitive constitution of dust and ashes. With the least tendency heavenward before his time, they tug him to earth at once.

These impertinent realists are the great destroyers of human happiness. They begin early, continue long, and never cease until the end of life. A mother's tenderness even can not soften their hard-hearted positivism. They will rudely blur the maternal vision of her child's beauty with the unwelcome assertion that it is ugly. "All babies are ugly," is a favorite proposition of these plain-spoken people. This may be a fact in natural history, but it is something that was never dreamt of in the philosophy of the mother to whom the ugliest child is most beautiful. In fact, as there are no absolute laws of beauty, there is no reason why the maternal fondness should not be accepted as the test in regard to the looks of her own infant. No indifferent person has the right to an opinion contrary to that of her who is so deeply concerned. A polite concurrence is the duty of every civilized being. Politeness, however, is never recognized as an obligation by the plain-spoken people, of one of whom we recollect an incident strikingly illustrative of this statement. A fond mother was displaying her first-born to a circle of her husband's friends. Among these there chanced to be a plain-spoken person of the plainest kind. Every one but him hastened to utter the compliment appropriate to the occasion. He kept what he had to say until the mother had been warmed to the highest point of maternal vanity by the intense expressions of admiration of all but him, when he deliberately dashed upon her this bucketful of cold water. "Your baby, madam," said he, "reminds me of a Flat-headed Indian." The comparison, it is true, was not inappropriate. As for the suitableness of the remark to the occasion, we leave it to all tender mothers to decide.

These plain-spoken people have the audacity to declare in the face of every boy that there never was such a person as Robinson Crusoe or his man Friday, and that Jack the Giant-Killer is a myth. Boys fortunately have a sturdy faith, sustained by a young and vigorous imagination, and they are generally proof to the unwelcome and improbable verities of plain-spoken people. It is, however, none the less cruel to torment the youthful credulity with the uncertainties of doubt.

Never invite a plain-spoken person to dinner, for he will be sure to detect the Newark cider in your Champagne bottle, and announce the fact before the whole company. Don't trust in his presence to the delusion of a wig, or confide in the artifice of a hair-dye, for he will penetrate the deceit, and expose you in all the baldness and grayness of age. After death, let not your family invite him to your funeral, for he will tell all your failings to his companion as he walks to your grave.

Plain-spoken people perhaps have their good side also. They are quick to detect every sham, and may serve as correctors of false pretension. If they would confine their detective propensities and their public denunciations to all the false shows of wealth, gentility, benevolence, and religion, we might wish them God-speed. While, however, they continue to run a muck at all the innocent illusions of the imagination and the heart, we shall keep our doors closed, and ourselves, if possible, secure from the shock of all plain-spoken people.

The prudishness which avoids calling things by their real names, "a spade *a spade*," etc., and resorts to all sorts of verbal device to escape the employment of some peculiar term become inexplicably offensive, is the worst form of immodesty, for it gives proof of impure thought, while it hypocritically strives to disguise it. We join with Sterne in his warning against the dangers of "accessory ideas." There are certain words peculiar to American usage which, so far from being recognized by the English, are unintelligible to them. There is not one man or woman in ten thousand of those who speak our language, except ourselves, who would understand what we mean by "rooster." We are gradually getting over, in this country, this false modesty of speech, and it is now perhaps possible to discover within a hundred miles of a metropolis an occasional pair of female lips capable of pronouncing "leg," "shirt," "body," or even "trowsers," and a face that will not redden at the remotest allusion to a subject more or less suggested by the presence of every reputable matron.

CHAPTER XI.

The Defects of the American Voice.—Their Cause.—Ugly Noises with the Mouth.—Decency of Motion.—Attitudinizing.—Affected Women.—Ugly Tricks.—Hand-shaking.—Democratic Intrusiveness.—American Publicity.—The Impertinence of British Loyalty.—Salutations.—Care of the Hands and Nails.

The American voice is generally more nasal and high-pitched than the English. Our women, particularly, are far less gentle and sweet-toned in speech than their British cousins. On hearing some of our damsels speak, we are forcibly reminded of the beautiful girl in the fairy-tale who could never open her mouth without letting out toads, vipers, and other ugly creatures. The sharpness of the American voice may possibly be somewhat due to the prevalent condition of the atmosphere in this country. This idea seems to be confirmed by the fact of a variation in tone according to the degree of latitude and longitude. The Northern and Eastern voices are certainly less soft than the Southern. Voice essentially depends upon hearing, and the sounds uttered will correspond pretty faithfully with the sounds heard. If these, in consequence of a clear, dry atmosphere, strike the ear shrilly, the vocal organs will naturally echo them in sharp, quick tones. Granting that the peculiar American voice may be greatly due to natural causes, we yet do not doubt that much can be done by care to qualify its monotonous harshness.

Our children, in accordance with their general freedom from restraint, are allowed to exercise their voices, as the rest of their franchises, without check. These "chartered libertines" accordingly use their tongues and lungs as those are wont who can do as they will with their own. They put them to the full stretch of their powers, and consequently shout when they should talk. Thus their utterance becomes habitually loud and impetuous, and necessarily shrill and monotonous, for high are sharp, and hasty are unmodulated tones. A little more rigidity of discipline in childhood would do much, we think, to correct not only the vocal, but some other defects of our people we might enumerate. Let our damsels bear always in mind that there is nothing so charming in woman as a low, sweet voice, and strive, accordingly, to evoke some variety and softness of tone from their vocal organs, which are not necessarily loud-sounding instruments of a single note, and that a sharp nasal one. The practice of reading aloud is a good means of learning to modulate the voice; and, in pronouncing each word, the mouth should be fairly opened, that the guttural sound may be heard, and not lost in a predominating nasal twang.

The mouth may offend by its inarticulate as well as articulate utterances. All unnecessary noises with this and its fellow-organ, the tongue, are fatal to decorum of manners. Humming, whistling, *hawking*, spitting, and sucking of the teeth are so disgusting that the mere mention of them seems almost an offense. Some folks, otherwise of passable manners, become insufferable whenever they attempt to take into their mouths fluids of any kind, which they never do without a succession of audible *flops.* This is generally a habit acquired in youth for want of proper direction. It would seem as if nothing were easier than to drink tea or eat soup without making an ugly noise, and yet there are few who seem capable of doing so. All that is necessary, in order to swallow a liquid with the quietness that decorum exacts, is to open the lips well, and to put the spoon fully into the mouth, should its use be necessary. All smacking of the lips, even over your host's finest Tokay, Consular Seal, or Burgundy, is but a barbarous mode of expressing an appreciation of vinous excellence, and had better be left to the drinkers of lager beer and "Bourbon" at the corner groggery.

The use of a toothpick of the proper kind is essential to a due care of the teeth, but should be no more exposed to public notice than any other necessary but unpleasantly suggestive article of the toilette.

Unlike those of some races, as the Oriental and the various Latin nations, the English and North American people do not show, in ordinary conversation, much flexibility of expression or movement. The best bred with us are apt to be composed, even to stiffness. A certain degree of action, provided it be always graceful, is not only consistent with, but absolutely essential to a decorous bearing. The "principal part of beauty," says Lord Bacon, "is in decency of motion." The face certainly, and the hands and arms, and even the whole body, more or less, should move in harmony with the discourse and sympathy with the general tone of conversation. In the interest of narrative and warmth of argument, considerable energy and variety of gesture are permissible, but the condition of grace must be exacted. We knew an emphatic talker, who was generally listened to with attention, and justly so, for he had often much to say to the purpose, and said it well, but whose action, though ordinarily not without grace, occasionally took a turn contrary to all the proprieties. In the height of conversation he would suddenly jump up, seize each tail of his faultless dress-coat, and, turning round and round like a whirling dervish, make such an unreserved revelation to all the company of his proportions, that modesty was shocked, and laughter could hardly hold its sides. The action was, of course, fatal to the eloquence it was intended to illustrate.

Ordinary people, who do not set up for brilliant talkers or powerful disputants, had better cultivate a uniform composure of manner. Let their bearing be easy and decorous, without laxity or stiffness.

To attitudinize, or *poser*, as the French term it, with the view of producing an impressive effect upon the beholder, seldom succeeds except with the rawest members of society. When detected, as it always is by accomplished people of the world, it creates, at first sight, a feeling of aversion which is not easy to eradicate.

This *posing* for effect is so old a trick, and so easy of detection, that it is surprising any person who has reached years of discretion should attempt to play it. Yet how often do we see it, in its various phases of the delicate young lady with the languid air, the listless step, or *die-away* posture!—the literary young lady, with the studiously neglected toilette, the carefully exposed breadth of forehead, and the ever-present, but seldom-read book!—the abstemious young lady, who surreptitiously feeds on chops at private lunch, and starves on a pea at the public dinner!—the humane young lady, who pulls Tom's ears and otherwise tortures brother and sister in the nursery, and does her utmost to fall into convulsions before company at the sight of a dead fly!—and the fastidious young lady, who faints, should there be an audience to behold the scene, at the sight of roast goose, but whose robust appetite vindicates itself by devouring all that is left of the unclean animal when a private opportunity will allow. We assure our young damsels that such affectations are not only absurd, for they are perfectly transparent, but ill bred, as shams of all kinds essentially are.

The management of the hands in company seems to embarrass young people greatly. This comes from the false modesty, or *mauvaise honte*, which induces them to suppose they are the observed of all observers. Let them think only of themselves in due proportion of estimate with the vast multitude of mankind, and frequent habitually the company of the refined, and they will probably overcome much of their awkwardness, if they do not acquire a large degree of grace.

There is nothing more annoying to other people who may be present than the noise which a person will sometimes make by snapping a toothpick, jingling a watch-chain, creaking a chair, opening and shutting a pencil or knife, tapping the boot with a cane, or making any kind of noise or movement which irresistibly and disagreeably attracts the general attention.

Every one should be particular to avoid acquiring in youth the habit of fumbling with any part of the person or thing appertaining to it. It is astonishing how fixed this may become. So completely are such habits, in cases of long practice, associated with the action of the person, that they seem to be incorporated into his very structure, as it were. There are people who, if suddenly deprived of the means of practicing some ugly and habitual trick, will be so paralyzed in brain and tongue as to be incapable of continuing a train of thought or current of speech. We knew a lawyer, learned in Blackstone, and an eloquent advocate, who had acquired the habit of twisting a piece of paper and twirling it between his fingers during his addresses to Court and jury. Whenever some roguish brother, as sometimes occurred, would take the opportunity of the speaker dropping the paper momentarily during a pause in his argument to remove it, his embarrassment became extreme. He stared anxiously around, fumbled every where with his fingers about the law books and briefs, stammered out a few incoherent words, blushed (for even he, lawyer as he was, would blush on such an occasion), and was entirely unable to collect his thoughts and renew his speech until some merciful comrade (probably the guilty brother) had restored to his hands its plaything, and to his mind and tongue their cunning.

It is well when these ugly tricks do not take the most offensive form; but occasionally we find persons, otherwise incapable of ill breeding, who will pick their noses, clean their nails, and scratch their heads before all kinds of company, and remain perfectly unconscious, from the insensibility of habit, of their offensive acts.

Hand-shaking is a national custom which we have in common with our English relatives from whom we derived it. In private intercourse they probably carry it to a greater excess than we, but on certain public occasions we practice it far more than they. Our sovereign people insist upon giving their Briarean hands to every domestic notability and distinguished foreign visitor. All the famous men from abroad who have become our national guests, from the Marquis de Lafayette to Kossuth, have been forced to submit to this manipulation by the universal democracy. Lafayette, with true French politeness, yielded gracefully to this demand for a touch of his glove by twenty millions of people, but he became very sparing of speech. He only asked of each one who came up, as he shook hands with him, "Are you a married man?" If the answer was "Yes," the marquis rejoined, "Happy fellow!" If the answer was "No," he exclaimed, "Lucky dog!" With this meagre luggage of nine words the economical marquis is said to have kept himself in ready English speech, and made a creditable appearance during his whole journey from Maine to Georgia. No makeshift, however, would avail him as a substitute for the giving of his hand, which, at the end of his triumphal march, was fairly shaken into a paralysis. This kind of hospitality to public men is more honored in the breach than the observance, for, expanding naturally with the wonderful increase of our population, it has finally become insupportably liberal. The intrusive curiosity to see and touch the great, to their manifest discomfort, is as far removed from decorum as reverence. Our public personages will be forced, before long, in self-protection, to resist this democratic intrusiveness. No popular favorite can physically endure to have his hand often shaken by forty million sturdy fellow-citizens, or even to bear pecuniarily the expense to which the thousands of gloves necessary to guard it must amount.

A president held in such reverence that he can safely resist the inordinate humors of the democracy should venture to reform the official manners of the nation. He could be surrounded without hedging himself, as doth a king, with more ceremonial observances, to the manifest increase of his own comfort and the improvement of the manners of his fellow-citizens. With all our informality, however, we have not yet reached that pertinacious intrusiveness of British loyalty which will follow the scent of queen, prince, or princess not only from the palace door through every street and over the whole country, but pursue it across seas, and throughout the width of the broadest continent.*

Personal reserve is far less easy of attainment in the United States than in most countries. Our

* It lately transpired that the Princess of Wales was about resorting for her health to the baths of Wildbad, in Würtemberg. To avoid being hunted up by a throng of eager pursuers, she slipped away disguised by an incognito; but, notwithstanding, her scent was caught, taken quickly up, and followed pertinaciously to her dinner-table in the little German town, where, at the last accounts, her subjects were quarreling over the cherry-stones ejected from the princely mouth.

political institutions, by their recognition of the equal rights of all men, call upon each individual to manifest himself. Every American being thus not only free to speak and act, but feeling it his duty to do so, becomes, more or less, a public man. The political influence extends to the social habits, and we have, in consequence, but little privacy of life.

Our love of publicity is shown by the gregarious modes in which we live and move. That great caravansary, the American hotel, is a characteristic expression of the national protest against individual separateness. It is constructed on the principle that it is not good for any human being to be alone except when he is asleep, and even then it is not seldom that he is provided with one or more companions. The bedrooms are made just large enough to lie down in, and are evidently only designed for that purpose. These, thrust far away under the eaves, are ordinarily the only provision for the individual. The rest, composing much the larger and most accessible part of the structure, is appropriated to the public, for whom, moreover, all the splendor and convenience are exclusively furnished. So much is the American hotel constructed for the especial advantage of the aggregate many, and so little are the requirements of the particular one considered, that, while thousands are feasted there luxuriously at certain hours every day, no single hungry man can, at any other moment, get a chop or a potato to save himself from starving.

In traveling the same gregarious practices obtain, and no one, however tender of body and fastidious in mind, can entirely escape the nudge of the elbow or the shock from the words of a rude neighbor.

This shaking together, so universal with us, has not been without its marked effects upon the character and manners of our people. The good may be thought by some to transcend the bad. It has led, undoubtedly, to a fuller recognition of common interests and mutual obligation, and thus humanized the multitude. Meeting together as we all do on the road and the road-side, in the enjoyment of the same cheaply-purchased privileges, we are forced, temporarily at least, to a social equality, which can not fail to elevate the spirit of the humble and check the aspirations of the proud.

One of the worst effects of the gregarious system is the perpetual intrusiveness of the many upon the retirement which is at times necessary and pleasing to each person. The uniformity of sentiment, moreover, which is apt to result, and overbear the private judgment and the individual conscience, may be also considered as one of the most serious evils. There is a certain boldness, too, of manners, which is more observable and offensive in the young than in others, which is traceable to the publicity of American life.

We should, particularly in this country, cultivate domestic privacy as the best check to the excessive tendency to gregariousness. We, on the contrary, are apt to cultivate the latter at the expense of the former; thus the practice common with us of living in hotels and boarding-houses, where that reserve so necessary to the development of the individual character and the acquisition of modest manners is impossible.

There will be always a publicity naturally resulting from our political and social institutions which can not be avoided. It behooves us, therefore, to augment its good and diminish its ill effects as far as it lies in our power. As we can not get rid of each other, let us make ourselves mutually useful and agreeable by the improvement of our sentiments and manners. With the greater publicity in America, public opinion is necessarily more extensive in its influence, and therefore it is especially important that it should be exerted in favor of the good and beautiful.

In private life in this country the hand is not

often given except to intimate friends and relatives. In England it is more freely extended to those met for the first time. Ordinarily it should be left to the older or more distinguished to make the proffer of the hand. Cavaliers and dames in this country, as in France, seldom extend to each other the hand unless there is a great difference of age and position, or much intimacy of relation. Whenever the hand is given, it is not necessary to draw off the glove, as some attempt to do, with a great deal of fuss and consequent embarrassment.

There is a great deal of tact required in adapting the salutation to the occasion. The mere nod, which is allowable, perhaps, between the comrades of a school and college, the "fellows" of an office, a counting-house and shop, or the cronies and "friends" of girlhood, should never be passed between courteous people of full growth and age. They should give an unequivocal bow or courtesy, which, however, women are not expected to stop when under full headway, and make according to the principles laid down by their last dancing-master. A graceful bend of the head and shoulders is all that is necessary. A gentleman will raise his hat fairly from the head, and not limit his salutation to a mere touch of the rim, like a coachman or a waiter. The salutation is made to suit the various degrees of intimacy by the accompanying expression of the face, which can indicate familiarity by a smile or look of conscious recognition, and reserve by a composed aspect and an indifferent glance. The variations are, however, not easily defined in words, though discerned without difficulty in action, and must therefore be left to the individual tact.

On meeting a friend in company with a lady, though a stranger, it is necessary to be very particular in giving the bow all its fullness and formality, that it may indicate respect for the dame, as well as intimacy with the cavalier. So, too, when two male friends walking together meet the female acquaintance of one, it behooves both to raise their hats.

It is common, in this country and in England, to await the recognition of the lady before bowing, though in France it is the reverse; but in the three countries, where the intimacy is great, the mutual salutation is ordinarily simultaneous.

When, in the park or public promenade, there is constant passing and repassing, it is found convenient to limit the formal recognition of an acquaintance to the salutation on first sight.

The chance meeting of a person at the house of a common friend, when there has been no formal introduction, is not considered a necessary reason for giving or expecting a salutation. Where either, however, bestows it, it should be courteously and fully returned. The French are more liberal of their courtesies than we and our reserved relatives in England. A Frenchman will take off his hat to any person he may meet on the outside steps of his own or a friend's house, as he thinks that the mere fact of this common relation to the same house, though it be transitory, establishes a bond of communion, however slight, demanding acknowledgment.

A lady seated in a room is not expected to rise from her chair when saluted by a gentleman or by one of her own sex unless the latter be a person very much her superior in age.

A bow should always be acknowledged, by whomsoever proffered, whether master or man, maid or mistress, unless there is a good reason and an intention to rebuke.

All salutations had better be omitted than given in a way to indicate an unwilling politeness. The clipped bow, the "mutilated courtesy," as Goldsmith calls it, and the incomplete shake of the hand, in which the scornful touch of two fingers is made to do service for a full grasp with the five, are odious mockeries of civility.

It would seem to imply a great distrust of the

nicety of man and womankind to suggest to them the necessity of keeping the hands and their appurtenances in good condition. These noticeable parts of the body are, however, often neglected or treated unbecomingly. The nails of people who boast to be fastidious in the care of their persons are not seldom far from being well cared for. Dean Swift was so nice in this respect that he used to cut his nails to the very quick to secure their freedom from uncleanliness of all kind. We do not advise this mode of preventing a very disgusting result, for a very short nail is not seemly.* It is an ugly practice, too, according to our notions, to let the nails grow until they lengthen into claws. It was, however, a fashion in France during the reign of Louis XIV. to cultivate a great length of the nail of the little finger, and this was for the purpose of being able to scratch at a door, which every visitor was expected to do, instead of knocking, when wishing to gain admittance to a fashionable friend. Molière speaks of "l'ongle long" that the marquis of his day "porte au petit doigt"—that is, of the long nail worn at the end of the little finger.

* The inner part of the nail should never be scraped with a file or cutting instrument, for this will produce a rough surface, in the irregularities of which the dirt will lodge, and be very difficult of removal.

CHAPTER XII.

Effect of Civilization on Dress.—The opposite Progress of Man and Woman in the Art of Dressing.—The true Rule of Dress.—Uniformity of Dress in America.—Inappropriateness of Dress.—Sunday-best.

Civilization has done little more for the human passion of personal adornment than extend, by its progress in the arts, the means of gratifying its barbaric caprices. The taste in dress of the Parisian dame of fashion is not essentially more refined than that of the Choctaw squaw. All the manufacturing and commercial triumphs of the nineteenth century are, it is true, more or less manifest in the complicated drapery of the one, while, in the scant covering of the other, every thing indicates the rudeness and simplicity of an artless nature. Hair cut from the head of a Hottentot woman, brought from remote Caffreland, purified by an elaborate chemical process of its native foulness, and turned by ingenious machinery into the fashionable headdress known as the *chignon*, implies great commercial enterprise, scientific skill, and mechanical ingenuity. These are undoubtedly among the forces to which civilized people owe their might and superiority to barbarians. The *chignon*, as a product, is unquestionably beyond the undeveloped resources of the whole Choctaw nation. Worn, however, as a head-dress, with its tumor-like excrescence and morbid deformity of proportion, it indicates in the woman of civilization no progress in taste beyond her barbaric sister of the American forest and prairie. The wild flowers and eagle feathers of the savage are, in fact, vastly more chaste and beautiful than the elaborate monstrosities worn by the civilized being.

There has been of late years a certain divergence between masculine and feminine taste in dress. Woman has been rapidly becoming more fanciful, artificial, elaborate, and expensive in costume, until she has finally reached such a frightful complexity of capricious finery, involved form, minute detail, various color, and accumulated material, that she appears but a confused bale of miscellaneous dry goods, upon which nothing is clearly indicated but the mark of the high price.

Man, on the contrary, has, in these latter days, with a great tendency to simplification of costume, finally reached what Carlisle, we believe, termed a series of pokes or sacks, loosely adapted to successive parts of the frame—a sack for the trunk, two sacks for the upper, and two for the lower extremities, which form a complete suit of masculine attire. There is, however, apparently a disposition on the part of the young *beaux* to fall back into the fantastic splendors of past time, and there may now be occasionally seen an increased elaborateness of make in the coat and trowsers, and showiness of display in the cravat, shirt bosom, and waistcoat. With all this, however, there is generally a commendable simplicity in men's attire. The change is immense from the laced ruffles, embroidered scarlet coats, and breeches of brilliant satin, silk stockings, and diamond buckles of our ancestors of a hundred and fifty years ago. Think of poor Goldsmith promising to pay—an obligation he was much more ready to assume than perform—£50, or two hundred and fifty dollars, a century ago, when money was much more valuable than at present, for his "suit of Tyrian bloom," in order to shine in the beloved eyes of the "Jessamy bride." Not twenty years since, so elaborately fabricated was the collar of a coat, that more labor and money were expended upon it than are now required to make and pay for a whole suit of clothes. Taste and convenience have gained much by the increased simplicity of man's costume, and it must be acknowledged that his plain garments, if they do not express so fully the progress of the arts as woman's rich habiliments, indicate, by their fitness, more certainly the advanced intelligence of the age than her superfluously elaborate but barbaric finery.

We are far from advising a general indifference to dress, however justifiable we might think the renunciation of some of the superfluities of modern female costume. Chesterfield, in urging upon his son a due attention to his clothes, says a man of sense "dresses as well, and in the same manner, as the people of sense and fashion of the place where he is. If he dresses better, as he thinks—that is, more than they—he is a fop; if he dresses worse, he is unpardonably negligent; but of the two, I would rather have a young fellow too much than too little dressed; the excess on that side will wear off with a little age and reflection; but," he adds, in a sentence which seems strong, coming from his perfumed presence, "*if he is negligent at twenty, he will be a sloven at forty, and stink at fifty years old.*"

His lordship, in continuing his advice, makes these sensible remarks: "Dress yourself fine where others are fine, and plain where others are plain; but take care always that your clothes are well made and fit you, for otherwise they will give you a very awkward air. When you are once well dressed for the day, think no more of it afterward, and, without any stiffness for fear of discomposing that dress, let all your motions be as easy and natural as if you had no clothes on at all."

It is a canon of good taste in dress, as well as in all other things, to avoid extremes. A person of taste will take care not to be the last to leave an old, or the first to assume a new fashion:

> "Be not the first by whom the new are tried,
> Nor yet the last to lay the old aside."

He will never be singular in his dress, for, like all well-bred people, he would escape special notice in his daily walks. It is on this account that he does not startle by a novelty, or excite curiosity by an antiquity of costume. He will, however, though avoiding in his dress what may force notice, be careful so to order it that, if by chance it should attract attention, it will be remarked for its taste and conformity with the observances of the refined. Such is considered decorous by the cultivated of both sexes, though women ordinarily do not allow themselves the same discretion as men in their fealty to fashion, which, however, in this country particularly, is too slavishly obeyed by both sexes, with the natural consequence that few of either are appropriately clothed.

The uniformity of dress is a characteristic of the people of the United States. The man of leisure and the laborer, the mistress and the maid, wear clothes of the same material and cut. Political equality renders our countrymen and countrywomen averse to all distinctions of costume which may be supposed to indicate a difference of caste. The uniformity which results is not favorable to the picturesque, and our every-day world in America has, in consequence, the shabby look of being got up by the Jews in Chatham Street, and turned out in a universal suit of second-hand clothing.

Our working-people, in vindicating their claims to social equality by putting on their heads the stove-pipe hat and flimsy bonnet, and clothing their bodies in tight-fitting coats and flowing robes, not only interfere with the picturesque, which is of minor importance, but make, we think, an unwise sacrifice of comfort, convenience, and economy. What could be more unfavorable to that free movement of the muscles essential to those trades and occupations requiring the exercise of physical force than the scant coat and tight-fitting trowsers now in vogue? It would be as well to put Hercules in a strait-jacket, and set him thus accoutred to slay the hydra, as for our muscular sons of labor to clothe themselves in suits of fashionable cut, and so to strive at their mighty work. It is surprising that the blouse of the French workman is not generally adopted. Nothing can be more graceful, convenient, and economical. Its lines are flowing, its form admits of perfect freedom of movement, and it can be made of a material both cheap and lasting. Artists generally adopt the blouse for work in their studios, and thus guarantee its tastefulness as well as utility. The free American citizen has no reason to scorn it as a symbol of slavery. The French blouse has vindicated its title to the drapery of a freeman in many a bloody encounter with tyranny on the barricades and in the streets of Paris.

As for the suitableness of the female dress of fashion to working-day purposes no one will venture, we suppose, to hold that crinoline is convenient in the china-closet or safe in the proximity of a red-hot stove, and that a flowing train of silk is the most appropriate broom for the kitchen floor. Crinoline and train, however, are constantly found in these inappropriate places and dangerous proximities. We can not for the world see why Bridget and Katarina, and their mistress too, indeed, when the occasion requires, should not dress appropriately—to their spheres we do not say, but to their occupations. They would be gainers in every respect—in taste, comfort, convenience, and economy. It is quite a mistake for the female servant to suppose that by spending her money in gaudy dress and mock finery she advances her social position, though with her rustling silk she may pass in the dark, or, coming out of the front-door on a Sunday, be taken at a distance for her mistress. She may spend a half year's wages on a flimsy bonnet, it will not avail her—the sham lady will still be manifest. If she has personal charms of her own and desires that they should be appreciated, let her take the advice of the tasteful, who will tell her that the rude freshness of natural beauty appears to the greatest advantage in a plain setting.

A white cap, a close-fitting jacket, with sleeves neither so tight as to hinder movement nor so loose as to lap up the gravy or sweep off the sherry glass, and a short skirt of simple stuff—plain or many-colored as it may be—make an appropriate costume for the household servant. Scraps of cotton lace, bits of bright ribbon, and collars and cuffs of linen, may be added according to the taste. Any one who has seen the picture of the Chocolate Girl of the Dresden Gallery will not doubt of the picturesque capabilities of a dress which was so effective in this particular instance that it procured a rich and titled husband for the original of the portrait.

The female cap should be insisted on as an essential to cleanliness by those who are not so sentimental as to prefer to receive daily pledges of the cook's affection in the shape of locks of hair in the soup.

We Americans are famous for putting our best foot foremost. This practice, however commendable on the whole, may be carried too far in particular instances. In our eagerness to make a good appearance we are apt to become too demonstrative. This shows itself in our talk, which is remarkable for its bold self-assertion; in our houses and furniture, which are made more to attract the eye of the stranger than to suit the taste of the possessor; and, above all, in our dress.

There are no such universally well-dressed people in the world as the Americans. It is not only that more of them than of any other nation have good clothes to their backs, but their garments are better made and adjusted to their persons, and worn with an easier grace. While this much may be allowed, it can not be denied that offense against taste and convenience of dress, particularly as to time and occasion, is frequent with us.

We are generally too finely got up for the occasion. We are apt to be, as the French say, *endimanchés*, which we may translate by the coined word *Sundayfied*. We often choose the wrong time for the display of our personal finery. For example, while the people of the most refined taste avoid all exhibition of rich dress and flaunting colors in church, we ordinarily turn the sanctuary into a show-room for the fashions. A well-bred French or English woman always chooses her most sober and unnoticeable dress in which to say her prayers in public, while an American puts on her newest robe and gayest bonnet to perform her genuflections before an admiring congregation of fellow-worshipers. The holiest day of the sacred calendar, Easter Sunday, would lose all its significance in the mind of one of our dames if unassociated with the inauguration of the spring fashions. She would no more think of bowing her head in prayer on such an occasion unadorned with the latest bonnet of the season, than walking up the church aisle on her knees.

We shall leave our gewgawed devotees to reconcile humiliation in worship with vanity of dress. That is a problem which we confess we have neither the right nor the capacity to solve. It must be left to the conscience of the bedizened worshiper, aided by the skillful casuistry of her theological director. How far fine clothes may affect the personal piety of the devotee we do not pretend even to conjecture, but we have a very decided opinion in regard to their influence upon the religion of others. The fact is, that our churches are so fluttering with birds of fine feathers that no humble fowl will venture in. It is impossible for poverty in rags and patches, or even in decent but simple costume, to take its seat, if it should be so fortunate as to find a place, by the side of wealth in brocade and broadcloth. The poor are so awed by the pretension of superior dress and "the proud man's contumely" that they naturally avoid too close a proximity to them.

The church being the only place on this side of the grave designed for the rich and the poor to meet together in equal prostration before God, it certainly should always be kept free for this common humiliation and brotherhood. It is so in most of the churches of Europe, where the beggar in rags and wretchedness and the wealthiest and most eminent, whose appropriate sobriety of dress leaves them without mark of external distinction, kneel down together, equalized by a common humiliation, before the only Superior Being. The adoption of a more simple attire for church on the part of the rich in this country would have the effect, certainly not of diminishing their own personl piety, but probably of increasing the disposition for religious observance on the part of the poor. Want of fine dress would no longer, as it is now, be the common motive for staying away from the house of worship, and these would become the common places of assemblage, as on the Continent of Europe, for the poor and the rich. The result would not only be favorable to general piety, but to social harmony, since the union of all classes on one day of the week, at least, would tend to level the artificial barriers of separation.

"The distinctions of civil life," says Paley, in one of his most admired passages, "are almost always insisted upon too much, and urged too far. Whatever, therefore, conduces to restore the level, by qualifying the dispositions which grow out of great elevation or depression of rank, improves the character on both sides. Now things are made to appear little by being placed beside what is great, in which manner superiorities, that occupy the whole field of the imagination, will vanish, or shrink to their proper diminutiveness, when compared with the distance by which even the highest of men are removed from the Supreme Being, and this comparison is naturally introduced by all acts of joint worship. If ever the poor man holds up his head, it is at church; if ever the rich man views him with respect, it is there; and both will be the better, and the public profited, the oftener they meet in a situation in which the consciousness of dignity in the one is tempered and mitigated, and the spirit of the other erected and confirmed."

The same want of adaptation of the dress to the occasion, as exhibited in female church costume, is shown by the habit prevalent among our dames of putting on their showiest garments whenever going out, even should it be for the performance only of the most ordinary duty connected with the household. Whether it is to the shop to buy a dozen kitchen towels, to the grocer's to dabble in butter, or to the butcher's to dribble in the blood of a sirloin, she is the same finely-dressed personage. She more frequently, however, avoids the inconsistency of performing humble duties in lofty attire by shifting them to the lowlier and more soberly-clad shoulders of her husband. This is one, and not the least, of the ill effects of this habit of female overdress. It unfits women for the simple and unostentatious duties of household life.

Our unmarried girls are entirely overdressed. They are allowed to wear such suits as are never worn by modest maidens in Europe, and are hardly seen in public upon the most matronly persons. The young miss, flauntingly costumed, is sure to attract a notice in the streets which should not be agreeable to, and is hardly safe for, virgin modesty.

Our countrywomen, as also our countrymen, are recognized immediately on the highways of travel by the finery of their dress. The glistening black coat and satin waistcoat, and the silk gown and flimsy bonnet of fashion, are discerned at once amidst the dust of the railway and the smoke of the steamer as American national peculiarities.

Apart from the obvious advantage on the score of economy of adapting the dress to the occasion, there are certain moral effects of higher importance which might be expected from a national reform in this particular. Overdress leads to false expectations, and confirms a deceitful vanity which prompts to pretense of wealth, and all the iniquitous means by which it may be supported. It has more to do than any other single cause with the fall of woman, the bankruptcy of husbands, and the ruin of families. Its effect in destroying female reserve, especially that of the young, as it thus takes away one of the best safeguards of virtue, makes it very pernicious.

The excess of dress is certainly the cause of much of the characteristic vice of the day; and with the general adoption of a more modest attire, there would be less temptation to that part, at least, of the prevalent ill doing for which women are responsible.

CHAPTER XIII.

Superfinery of Dress.—Overdressed Women.—Slatterns at Home. —Hygiene of Dress.—Child-hardening.—Its Cruelty and Folly.—Stove-pipe Hats and Dress-coats.

WHILE neatness and propriety are always obligatory, and richness may be occasionally allowed, superfinery of dress is never permissible. This is, indeed, so far relative, that what may be regarded as excessively ornamental or expensive for one person, may be only plain or even mean for another. If there are to be fine people who are neither to toil nor to spin, it may be proper that they should be set off with fine array. They, as the lay figures, the male and female manikins upon which Fashion hangs her tinsel stuffs, variegated streamers, and showy gewgaws, may be indispensable as society is now constituted. These, whatever superincumbent finery they may sustain, are only fulfilling their vocation, but ordinary people are not called upon to submit to the same oppressiveness of splendor.

People of nice taste will strive at a certain

uniformity of dress. They will not be all shabbiness to-day and finery to-morrow, but, while adapting their attire to the occasion, will avoid both extremes, and thus be always decorously dressed.

It is the overdressed dame of the promenade and drawing-room who is the most apt to be the slattern of the domestic parlor and nursery. The woman who makes a point of dressing, as she calls it, for company, is generally very indifferent to the aspect she presents at home. With her there is no decent mean between dress and undress, the stiffness of formality and the laxity of negligence. She is like the tragedy queen of the play-house—a splendid sovereign before the foot-lights, and a dirty drab behind the scenes.

The moderately dressed woman, on the contrary, generally makes a uniform appearance of becoming neatness. Guided by good taste and sense, she dresses for home, knowing that what is decorous there will be always presentable to any company elsewhere. There are many wives of a fashionable tendency who presume too much on marital indulgence or indifference. These think that, after having caught their birds with chaff, they may throw it to the winds; but birds thus taken are only to be kept by a continued supply. Any woman who, after having won a husband by her fashionable airs, expects to retain his affections by a careless indifference to her appearance at home, will find out probably her mistake, and, it is to be hoped, before it may be too late.

The most fatal error a woman can make is to presume thus far upon her privileges as a wife. No man can long endure a slattern at home, and especially if she appears the fine lady abroad, and thus shows her contemptuous preference of the opinion of others to his.

Women of moderate means, instead of concentrating their pecuniary forces upon this or that showy and expensive article of toilette, in order to dress for company, while they remain in a shabby negligence at home, would do more wisely to provide themselves with an abundant and decorous household wardrobe. A wise and true wife will take care that her house shall always wear an aspect cheerful and alluring to her husband. Men confess to the weakness, if a weakness, of being greatly attracted and influenced in their disposition to love by the mere dress of woman. Fielding, who had a wife whom he loved, and who was altogether worthy of his love, says of her, in that minute portraiture of her charms in his "Amelia," that with the assistance of a little girl, who was their only servant, she managed to dress the dinner, and likewise "dressed herself as neat as any lady who had a regular set of servants could have done." This charming woman was also equally attentive to every other domestic duty. She took as much pleasure in cooking "as a fine lady generally enjoys in dressing herself for a ball." She, moreover, "never let a day pass without instructing her children in some lesson of religion and morality; by which means she had, in their tender minds, so strongly annexed the ideas of fear and shame to every idea of evil of which they were susceptible, that it must have taken great pains and length of habit to separate them." Neatness and order in the personal dress of the housewife are thus generally accompanied by regularity and completeness in the performance of every domestic duty.

To appear well dressed in the eye of the man requires no great outlay of money, for it is notorious that he prefers the elegance of simplicity to all the display of expensive art. The neat maid thus is not seldom more to his taste than the showy mistress. He asks only for neatness, fitness, and harmony of color. If women dressed only to please him, they might dispense with nine tenths of the expenditure upon their toilettes. But women dress to please—we were going to, but should rather say, displease—each other, for their main object seems to be to provoke the envy of their sisters by an impossible costliness of attire.

A not uncommon evil of the love of finery in dress is the disregard to which it leads of the comfortable and wholesome. The absurd, tight-fitting black cloth dress suit is worn in midsummer, and the ballroom robe of gauze in the coldest winter. Many a delicate frame shivers beneath a flimsy and imperfect covering, which is only put on because it is conformable with some capricious idea of becomingness. Fashion, by her reckless disregard of the laws of nature and health, has sent hecatombs of her most faithful devotees to premature graves. The hygiene of dress is a subject which has been much neglected, but deserves to be thoroughly studied.

In this country, deriving our fashions as we do from regions in a different latitude and hemisphere from our own, we seldom wear, in any division of the year, the clothes suitable to the season. The winter garments, especially of our women and children, are seldom warm enough.

The philosophy of dress is not difficult to master, for all that is required for the purpose is the application of a few of the elementary laws of chemistry.

The popular notion that the body receives warmth from the covering, whatsoever it may be, that is put upon it, is, according to science, an error. All the heat we have is of our own making, and is the result of the perpetual combustion going on in us and every living animal. The fat of what we eat, being chiefly carbon, or charcoal, supplies the fuel, and the oxygen of the air we breathe may be considered the fire which burns it. Scientifically, however, it is the act of combination of these two elements—carbon and oxygen—which constitutes the combustion from which results the heat of our bodies.

The only purpose of dress, apart from satisfying the demands of decency and fashion, is to facilitate or prevent the escape of the natural warmth of the animal system. In summer we accordingly try to get rid of it, and in winter, on the contrary, we strive to retain it. The former is done by covering the body lightly with such materials as favor, and the latter by clothing ourselves heavily with such textures as oppose the passage of heat. The dress of summer is accordingly of thin, close texture, ordinarily white in color, and composed of cotton or linen. That of winter is of a thick, loose texture, generally black or dark, and made of silk and wool. This, which is the result of the experience of ages, accords in every respect with the principles of science.

Chemistry divides substances into conductors and non-conductors of heat. Tissues of close, thin texture, such as cotton and linen, are good conductors, and thus are suitable for summer dress, as they conduct away or carry off rapidly the warmth of the body. Thick, loose textures, made of wool or silk, are, on the other hand, *non*, or bad conductors, and do not conduct away or carry off rapidly the animal heat, and are thus adapted to clothing the body in winter.

Dr. Franklin's experiment proves that color has a decided influence upon the absorption of solar heat. He spread several pieces of cloth of varied tints upon the snow exposed to the warmth of the sun, and found that the snow beneath the black melted the most rapidly, and that below the white the least so. Whenever the wearer is exposed to the rays of the sun, he will find a black dress hotter than a white one. In winter, accordingly, he will do well to choose the former, and in summer the latter.

The make as well as the material of the dress has a great deal to do with its warmth. The atmosphere is the worst of all conductors of heat. Accordingly, a loosely-made garment, which in its various folds incloses an abundance of air, must necessarily be a greater obstacle to the escape of the warmth of the body than a close-fitting dress. The non-conducting power of woolen and other loose fabrics is mainly owing to the large interstices of the tissue being filled with air.

A loose dress is, moreover, warmer, because it admits of the free circulation of blood, while a tight one impedes it by constricting the vessels, and thus hindering that free supply of the element essential to keeping up the brisk combustion upon which depends the due heating of the body.

Winter clothing, then, to be warm, should be of thick, loose texture, as cloth, flannel, and other woolen stuffs, dark in color, and of a cut so flowing that it may embrace within its folds stratum upon stratum of non-conducting air, and so loose as not to pinch any where, whatever may be the motion of the body.

The rigid application of the arbitrary laws of fashion to children's dress is worse than an absurdity—it is a cruelty. It is obvious that the very young are entirely indifferent to, if not absolutely unconscious of the distinctions of costume, and that they care nothing for the cut or the stuff of a smock or a vest provided their limbs and bodies are at ease, and free to bend and move. Mothers dress children to gratify their own vanity, and are not seldom entirely regardless of their little ones, whose health and comfort they so frequently sacrifice. The fashionable style of children's costume is often singularly inappropriate. Much of it seems to have been devised in accordance with the prevalent notion that children can be hardened, as it is called, or rendered insensible, by exposure to the effects of weather. This is a vulgar error, and a dangerous one. Those who hold to it will point triumphantly, in proof of their opinion, to those rugged offspring of poverty, occasionally seen, who, in spite of their nakedness, seem to defy the cold and the storm. These, however, are the few of the many that disease has left untouched; they are the hardy plants which remain in the wastes of misery unwithered and undestroyed by the neglect and pestilence which have decayed and killed most of those of kindred growth.

It is a well-established fact that a much larger number of the children of the poor and miserable suffer from disease and die than of those of the rich and luxurious. The offspring of misery who survive are mostly the fortunate few endowed with an inherent vigor of constitution which is proof against the severest trials. None but the strongest children of poverty are left.

The weakest scion of wealth is often nurtured by care to health and long life. Luxury may not always make the most rational use of its opportunities in the bringing up of its fortunate offspring, but it has nothing to learn from misery in the forced neglect of its unhappy progeny, except that the health and life of the young are only to be preserved by the most careful tending.

The surface of the body can not, as is often supposed, be hardened by continued exposure to cold or intemperate weather of any kind. The skin, when in a wholesome condition, is soft and moist, and, moreover, is being constantly renewed, so that, whatever may be the age of the animal, its integument is always fresh and young. It thus constantly preserves its tenderness and its sensibility to changes of temperature and other impressions. It is true that certain parts of the skin, as that in the palm of the hand of the manual worker, does thicken and become hard. This, however, is not a natural state; and if by any process the whole surface of the body were covered with a similar shell of callousness, its vitality would probably be destroyed. It is necessary for the skin to retain its porousness and moist pliability in order to perform the function of transpiration which is essential to life. On some festive occasion or other, in Paris, the skin of a child was covered with gold-leaf, and died, in consequence, a few hours after, within its stiff and impervious shroud of gilt.

The inherent delicacy of the skin renders it particularly sensitive to cold and drafts of air. It therefore requires protection. The low-necked, short, and sleeveless dress, by which fond mothers delight to show off the swelling busts and rounded limbs of their darlings, is, accordingly, a vanity which can not be indulged in with safety in all latitudes and all seasons. During our severe winters there should be no part of the surface of the body of a child, with the exception of its face, exposed to the external air. With, however, the fiery furnaces, and the more than tropical heat of most of our prosperous interiors, the indoor clothing may be very light, or almost nothing, provided the temperature be uniform, and all drafts and changes of air be avoided. With the prevailing practice of overheating our houses, there is always, on going out, a danger in facing the winter's breath. To escape this, the greatest possible difference should be made between the indoor and outdoor clothing. This is obviously to be done by relying for warmth chiefly upon the cloaks and coats, pelisses, fur capes, and the exterior garments which are easily put on and off. If the under-clothing, or that ordinarily worn inside of the house, be too heavy, that put on on going out is apt to be too light to protect the body against the difference of temperature, which is the chief danger to be guarded against.

Of course, as air and exercise are essential to the health of the young, they must face the stern winter of their native land, but it is a fatal mistake to suppose that either nature or habit can render them insensible to its withering breath. The only security is in warm clothing, which must not be neglected with any absurd idea of *child-hardening*.

It is quite certain that some of the ordinances of fashion are in accordance neither with grace, convenience, nor health, and yet few will venture to refuse compliance with them. What can be uglier and more painful to wear than a stiff *stove-pipe* hat? and yet there is hardly any one in London below a peer of the realm, or above a costermonger's man, who will dare to show his head in the streets without such a covering. The black coat and white cravat *de rigeur* none of us must venture to dispense with on certain occasions, and yet how ugly! They have, moreover, the disadvantage of confounding master and man. The Paris *Figaro* gives us an illustration: "The other day a gentleman in this equivocal suit presented himself, with a package under his arm, at the door of the celebrated *modiste*, Madame W——. The porter, taking him by the cut of his coat for one of his own set, showed him up by the servants' staircase. He took the way indicated, and, after handing to madame a diamond head-dress to be altered, said, 'My wife being unable to come, I have brought it myself. Pray do it as soon as possible, and don't disappoint her.' As he was leaving, he added, 'I must congratulate you, madame, upon the excellent arrangement of your establishment,' and explained how he had been shown up by the kitchen way. The *modiste* was in a terrible rage at her porter, for the servant, as he had supposed, was no less a personage than the great Monsieur Rouher, the prime minister of imperial France, who had undertaken, when in full dress for dinner, a commission for his wife."

CHAPTER XIV.

Food.—Importance of the Manner of eating Food.—The Decency of Feeding.—Its Effect on Health and Appetite. —Chatted Food.—Dainty Feeders.

THE first essential is to catch our hare, and the second to cook it well, but the third is undoubtedly to eat it properly. A regard to the kind of food is hardly more necessary to its enjoyment and to health than the manner of eating it. There is no country in the world where there is such an abundance of good raw material for the supply of the dietetic necessities of man, or where there are so many people with the means of obtaining it, as in the United States. It may be added that there is hardly a nation that derives so little enjoyment and benefit as the American from its resources. These, which are so plentiful with us, and, if properly used, calculated to bestow so much pleasure and physical good, give a great deal less of either than the meagre supplies of less productive countries. Our abundance of food, so far from being a benefit, is made, by perverse use, an injury. We have so much that we undervalue it, and deem it unworthy of the care which is necessary in its preparation for wholesome nutriment. We thus confine ourselves mostly to the grosser articles of diet, or such as are ordinarily called plain food, and which require but little art to adapt them to the taste.

We are entirely too carnivorous in this country. We feed too exclusively on steaks of beef, chops of mutton, cutlets of veal, and joints of meat. All our dishes being what the French call pieces of resistance, the national stomach is kept in a constant state of active assault. This overstrains its energy, and produces that malady so common with us which the doctors call atonic dyspepsia; that is, the indigestion which arises from weakness in consequence of overwork.

The physiologists tell us that the human system requires for its proper nutrition a variety of food. There must be a due proportion of oily, albuminous, and saccharine matter to render the diet of man wholesome. Neither bread, meat, nor sugar, however necessary as a part of the whole, is sufficient alone to sustain the health and vigor of man. There must be a proper quantity of each in every daily meal. The experience of good livers, with their regular succession of courses of soup, fish, meat, vegetables, and dessert, has long since settled this matter of variety of food to their own satisfaction, and in accordance with the teachings of science. Our country friends are apt to scorn all lessons from such a quarter, but we assure them that in regard to their manner of eating they may follow the example of the fashionable with advantage. We know of nothing more dangerous to health than the higgledy-piggledy tables of our country cousins, where flesh, fowl, fish, and all the productions of the earth are mingled together in a confusion that perplexes the taste, and prevents all discrimination of choice. To eat such meals requires the voracity which rustic labor can alone give, and to digest them demands such a stomach as nature refuses to man, but grants, it is said, to the ostrich.

It is always well to begin the dinner as every Frenchman does—with soup. This quiets the excessive craving of the stomach, but does not completely satisfy the hunger; and by thus subduing its voracity, prevents it from inordinate indulgence in food that is less easy of digestion. So also is there a good reason why the sweet things should be eaten at the close of the dinner. All saccharine food has the effect of quickly satiating, and, if taken at the commencement of a meal, would satisfy the appetite so completely as to indispose it for the other more substantial articles of diet necessary to the proper nourishment of the body.

Human beings were never intended to be the mere guzzlers of food that they too often are. Though our animal appetites are a possession that we have in common with brutes, we are able, but they are not, to temper their grossness with the refinements of art.

This power, which is a distinguishing feature of man, is less often exercised than it should be, and we consequently find the human animal eating and drinking in a manner which gives indication only of the brutal instinct. There is nothing more suggestive of a piggery at swill-time than an ordinary "bar-room and restaurant" at the hours of luncheon. In what is swallowed on these occasions the human exercises no more discrimination than the porcine animal. As the former, with his head and elbows over the slushy bar, gulps down the "slings and cobblers," and other mysterious compounds of miscellaneous mixture, or bolts the indefinite oyster stews and clam chowders, how like he is to the latter, with his nose and fore feet in the overflowing trough of swill!

The combination on each plate of the numerous items of the hotel or boarding-house bill of fare, which passes daily the unquestioning swallow of American voracity, is a prodigious test of the powers of digestion. The result can not be otherwise than derangement of the functions of the stomach, disease of that organ, and consequent weakness of the whole body.

A due attention to the grace and decency of feeding is often the surest means of provoking the taste of the nice. A well-presented meal will entice the languid appetite when the same food ill served will repel all desire. This is a fact to be considered in the treatment of the sick, when weakness and delicacy make them especially fastidious. Those who have had any experience in their management know how great is the effect of a minute attention to the manner in which food or medicine is presented to them. The dose seems to lose much of its nauseousness when swallowed from the well-polished silver spoon, and the morsel of food neatly cut and orderly presented acquires a finer flavor. The connoisseur of wine would fail to catch the vague *bouquet* of the rarest sherry and finest Champagne if he drank them out of an earthen pot instead of the delicately blown glass.

In regard to eating, parsimony is by no means the best economy of time. There may be an immediate gain in hurrying through the daily repast, but the future loss, from ill health and premature death, will be far greater. It is particularly necessary to lengthen the American dinner, and we know of no better means of doing this than by dividing it into courses, and interposing between them cheerful interludes of social talk. A full hour at least should be spared from the busiest day for the main repast. It should never be slurred over by any of the miserable pretexts of the bar-room, eating-house, or confectionery, but treated with all the substantial consideration its importance demands. Let each one make the most of his dinner, whatever it may be. Let it be prolonged, and freed from grossness by a graceful ceremony; and, above all, let it be partaken of in company, for nothing is so depressing to mind and body as solitary feeding.

"A man's body and his mind are like a jerkin and a jerkin's lining: rumple the one, you rumple the other." The physiological fact, thus aptly and humorously illustrated by Sterne, is nowhere more apparent than in the mutual influence of digestion and mental emotion. Both the brain and stomach must be at ease for either to perform its functions properly. Cheerfulness of mind is as essential to a good digestion as a good digestion is essential to cheerfulness of mind.

The sudden announcement of bad news, or the occurrence of any thing to disquiet the mind, will not only arrest the hunger of the sharpest appetite for the choicest food, but produce a loathing of it. To eat, if it were possible, in such a state of mental discomfort, would be sure to result in a fit of indigestion, if not in something more serious.

When the stomach is satisfying its appetite, the mind should not only be free from any painful emotion, but in a state of gentle and cheerful excitement. "Chatted food," according to the old proverb, "is half digested." This suggests the advantage of social eating, than which nothing is more conducive to the enjoyment as well as the digestion of food. With the sociability of a mixed dinner company there comes just the degree of mental liveliness required. The mind is distracted from its own preoccupations by the common talk to which each one contributes, without making an exhaustive draught upon his resources. Thus there is general animation without any individual fatigue. The whole nervous system is, by this agreeable means, stirred to a gentle excitement, which is favorable to the performance of every bodily function, and especially to that of digestion.

Believing that sociability is an essential element of not only the enjoyable, but digestible dinner, we protest emphatically against solitary feeding, which is both a gross and unwholesome practice. It is, however, very general among our men of business. These have the habit of eating while they work. Although they drop the pen in assuming the knife and fork, their brains remain busy with their debit and credit calculations, without, however, taking into account what is due to health. They rush in the anxious interval between an offer and a sale or purchase to the trough of some neighboring bar-room. Here they fill their stomachs in the shortest time with the largest quantity of sludge —for the confused mess of stew, chowder, pie-crust, and other miscellaneous grub hardly deserves any other name—and hasten back to pronounce the last word of a bargain, which they have been ruminating while bolting their dinner. The bargain may turn out a good operation, but the dinner will be sure to be a losing, and, if often repeated, a fatal one.

Many of our over-refined dames seem to have adopted Lord Byron's notion, that eating is unbecoming to woman. It is a marvel how some of them manage to keep body and soul together with the apparent regimen of starvation to which they subject themselves. To see them at table, you would hardly think them capable of the solitary pea to which Beau Brummell confessed.

"Do you eat vegetables?" he was asked. "I once ate a pea," was his answer. Our delicate dames appear to have reduced themselves to the fabulous abstemiousness of the single blade of grass to which the old woman had gradually brought her cow.

At the regular repasts of the day the would-be genteel woman never seems to be hungry. She takes her place at the table apparently only as a matter of form, and handles her knife and fork with the same lackadaisical air of indifference as she would her painted fan at the Opera. She may possibly sip a spoonful of soup, or swallow an occasional crumb of bread, to pass the time; but of the substantials of beef and pudding she does not take enough to "choke a daw withal." Breakfast, dinner, and tea are no better than so many Barmecide feasts as far as she is concerned, and she might as well, for all she apparently eats, take her seat at the illusive board of Sancho Panza in Barataria.

It is hardly the genteel thing, perhaps, but we shall nevertheless venture to say to our lady friends, as Petruchio said to Katharine, "I know you have a stomach." Granting the fact of the possession of this important organ by women, we do not see why the genteelest of them should be ashamed of acknowledging it, and frankly doing what may be necessary to secure it in all its integrity. There is only one way of doing this, and that is filling the stomach at regular periods with plenty of wholesome food.

In former times the most distinguished and refined of women were hearty feeders, and, without any of the sneaking delicacy of modern days, made no scruples of handling a vigorous knife and fork before the whole world. Queen Elizabeth and her maids breakfasted on great rounds of beef, washed down with full tankards of strong beer. "My lord and lady," records an observer of the habits of the Earl of Northumberland and his countess, "have for breakfast at seven o'clock a quart of beer, as much wine, two pieces of salt fish, six red herrings, four white ones, and a dish of sprats." The Duchess of Orleans, the mother of the famous regent, while in the full enjoyment of the luxury of Versailles, in the time of Louis XIV., wrote: "A good dish of sour-krout and smoked sausages is, in my opinion, worthy of a king, and there is nothing preferable to it; a soup made of cabbage and bacon is more to my taste than all the delicate kickshaws they make so much of here." It is not astonishing that there were strong women in those days, such as the stout wife of a Duke Ernest of Austria, who could crack the hardest nut with her fingers, and drive a tenpenny nail home with her fist. And the Duchess of Orleans was wont to follow the hounds from morning until night, had been in at the death of more than a thousand stags, and had many a serious fall. "But," she says, "of the twenty-six falls from my horse that I have had, I have been seriously injured but once." Such was the toughness engendered by sour-krout, smoked sausage, and cabbage-soup!

There is very little doubt that much of the debility and disease so common among the women of our day is due to this genteel squeamishness in regard to substantial food. It is not that they absolutely starve themselves to death, for many of the most abstemious at the open dinner are the most voracious at the secret luncheon. Thus that fastidious dame, whose gorge rises before company at the sight of a single pea, will on the sly swallow cream tarts by the dozen, and caramels and chocolate-drops by the pound's weight. Women should know that health is not possible with a daily glut of bonbons and pastry, but that physiology teaches, and experience confirms, the necessity of a various and substantial diet, such as is supplied at the three regular meals of a well-ordered household. Let our dames get over their false shame of a vigorous use of the social knife and fork, and learn that in rejecting publicly beef and pudding, and devouring confectionery privately, they are in reality gross, and not dainty feeders.

CHAPTER XV.

Etiquette of the Breakfast.—Etiquette of the Luncheon.—Etiquette of the Dinner.

BREAKFAST—we mean the genuine breakfast, not the *déjeûner à la fourchette*, or luncheon—is the least ceremonious of meals. By common consent, many of the usual table formalities are dispensed with on this occasion. Though, in a well-regulated family, for the sake of inculcating order and punctuality, the attendance of each member may be required at a fixed hour, there is generally a wide discretion left to every one else in regard to the time of his sitting down to breakfast.

At this informal repast each person is left free, within certain limits, to consult exclusively his own convenience. In the great country houses of Europe, where a very ceremonious hospitality is kept up, the breakfast is deemed so far an exception to the general law of strict observance that it is served to the guests, as it might be to so many travelers at an inn, at any hour of the morning, in the dining-hall, or even in their own rooms.

It is not expected that there should be a gathering in the drawing-room or elsewhere of the whole party, and a simultaneous movement to the breakfast-table. The well-marshaled procession usual at dinner may be and is generally dispensed with. The distinctions of rank and age are not recognized, and the laughing child may take precedence of the gravest dignitary. Each one, in fact, is allowed to drop in when and how he may. The presence of even the host and hostess is not exacted, although, where there is a household of children requiring the discipline of order and punctuality, no parent should fail to set the example of regular observance of the hour of breakfast, as of every other meal.

The breakfast-table should be, in accordance with the unceremoniousness of the repast, very simply dressed. The damask table-cloth and napkins, the service of white china, the shining urn or kettle, the pat of butter with its crystal of ice, the crisp loaf, and the glistening vessels of glass symmetrically arranged, have in themselves a freshness very enticing to a morning appetite. The oval table is both more pleasing to the eye and convenient for use. The centre should always be adorned with flowers if they can be obtained, or by fruit when in season. The dame of the house takes her place at the head or the side of the table, and before her she has the tray with the various vessels for preparing the usual domestic beverages—tea and coffee. These, to be good, should be made up stairs just before they are served. The old-fashioned urn, which was a huge, ugly, funereal thing, darkening the whole table with its solemn bulk, and eclipsing the blooming face of the matron, has given way, fortunately, to a more graceful tea-kettle of bronze. This should be placed on the table in front or at the side of the tray, and may be kept boiling during the whole meal by means of its alcoholic lamp. The hot water should be freely used, not so much to temper the tea and coffee as to rinse out the cups. The slop-bowl is, moreover, a necessary vessel, which, however, is too often wanting. Fastidious people don't care to see the *jetsons* and *flotsams* of their first cups floating in their second. We need hardly say that Dr. Johnson's mode of helping the sugar is not recognized by nice people as the proper one, any more than it was by Mrs. Thrale, who, as we recollect, ordered the bowl to be taken away after the learned lexicographer had dipped his inky fingers into it. The old fellow, it is true, took this lesson of cleanliness very ungratefully, and threw, with a demonstrative but illogical spite, one of Mrs. Thrale's best china cups into the fire, saying that if the one vessel was unfit for use after his fingers had been in it, the other, once touched by his lips, was equally so. In France, where they are not always as reserved in the use of their hands as they might be, the dames not seldom thrust them into the sugar-basins. This French fashion we can not recommend for adoption into this country.

It is not customary for fastidious people to accept of more than two cups of tea or coffee; but we do not know why good breeding, though moderation and temperance in all things is one of its cardinal principles, should confine itself precisely to that number. Dr. Johnson used to take a score or more at a single sitting. It has always been recognized as a symbol—the origin of which we do not pretend to know—of having had enough when the drinker leaves his spoon in the tea or coffee *cup*, and of his wanting more when it is left in the *saucer*. We would advise, however, our hospitable dames not to rely too much upon such indications. It is a convenience, and is, moreover, the fashion, first set, it is said, by no less a personage than Queen Victoria, to place the whole loaf of bread on the table, with a large knife by its side; and this, we may say, is the only occasion when this instrument should be used. The bread with which each one is served ought always to be broken, and never cut.

The breakfast to suit a morning appetite, which, though in a healthy person always brisk, is somewhat unsophisticated, should be composed of light and easily-digestible food. Nothing is more suitable, therefore, than a farinaceous diet. Bread, of course, in its various forms, must constitute the staple; but, in addition to these, the usual preparations of hominy and buckwheat are excellent breakfast articles. Butter and molasses with such food—the free use of which it is not uncommon to prohibit to children—fulfill, according to chemistry, an essential part in the economy of digestion and nutrition. Milk should always constitute a large proportion of the morning meal, not only of children, but of adults. Much of the vigor of muscle and brain of the Scotch has been attributed to their free use of oatmeal porridge and pease brose mixed with milk.

We are no great advocates for a solid meat diet at the first meal of the day. In frosty weather, a rasher of bacon, a sausage or two conscientiously made, some whitefish, or a slice of cold meat, may be well, but the hot steaks and chops had better be postponed for the more deliberate repasts. When cold meats, game, and meat pies, the remnants of a previous feast, form part of the breakfast, it is considered good taste to banish them to the sideboard. The hacked joint or the ragged pastry of the day before would certainly not harmonize with the delicate freshness and neatness of a well-set breakfast-table. Eggs and fruit in their seasons are always proper. In fact, the latter is more suitable food in the earlier than in the latter part of the day. The old proverb says, "Fruit is gold in the morning, silver at noon, and lead at night."

It is always considered good breeding to get through the breakfast with as little formality of service as possible. The well bred on such occasions, whatever force they may have of flunkies, dispense as far as possible with their presence, and content themselves with a neatly-attired and unobtrusive maid or a retiring valet, who knows when to make a timely exit.

The simplest costume is always regarded as the most becoming at breakfast. The matron should make her appearance in white cap and early-morning indoor dress; and the master of the house may present himself almost as he will, even in a shooting-jacket, but never in morning wrapper or slippers. These are too suggestive of the sick-chamber. We incontinently put our fingers to our noses when we see them.

The luncheon, which the etymologists would persuade us is derived from *clutch* or *clunch*, and should be consequently spelled *clutcheon* or *cluncheon*, meaning simply a handful of food, has lost much of its primitive signification. The modern luncheon is no longer regarded by those who know how to live as a mere sop to be thrown to that hungry Cerberus of the stomach, the appetite, with the view of quieting only for a moment its growlings, but a deliberate, satisfying meal.

The modern luncheon of our people is the *déjeûner à la fourchette*—the breakfast with a fork—of the French.

> "What a breakfast! Oh, not like your ghost
> Of a breakfast in England, your curs'd tea and toast!"

Under the old name of luncheon most thriving and well-regulated families daily sit down to the Frenchman's *déjeûner à la fourchette.* When the first breakfast, which we suppose and recommend to be a light, farinaceous one of bread or hominy, with milk, tea, or coffee, has been taken at eight in the morning, the more substantial second or luncheon should be eaten about four hours or so afterward—say at twelve or half past twelve o'clock. The interval, however, between two solid meals can be prolonged to six hours.

It is customary to make the luncheon servè

the double purpose of a second breakfast for the grown-up members of the family, and an early dinner for the children and servants. It is essential that the young should eat their main repast early in the day, for, if it were postponed until its close, they would be constantly exposed to the danger of going to sleep with a full stomach. The attempt to keep a child awake beyond his natural hour for repose is seldom practicable, and always cruel. At the same time, if by any mischance or bad management he is gorged with food at a late hour, it is hardly safe to put him to bed. There is no more frequent cause of the serious and sudden ailments of children than yielding to the somnolency of satiety.

Thrifty housekeepers often make the luncheon out of the remains of the previous day's dinner. This, however, can be carried too far, for it must be borne in mind that no *réchauffé* or rehash has the nutritious qualities of a fresh dish. Growing children should not be restricted to vapid remnants, but occasionally, at least, be regaled with newly-cooked and juicy meat. The luncheon is apt to be made of a disproportionate quantity of dessert and sweets. These are often used by well-meaning thrift to piece out the natural scantiness of a meal composed of the leavings of the day before. Plain puddings and pastry, when kept in proper subordination to the more nutritious diet of meat and vegetables, will injure no one, man or child, but they are superfluities, and should never be allowed to take the place of necessaries.

Of late years the luncheon, or *déjeûner à la fourchette*, has been dignified by its formal recognition by society as a ceremonious repast. Our men of business are too sparing of their time to give an hour pledged to trade to the delights of a social breakfast. They accordingly content themselves with "slings" and "chowder," which can be gulped down in a breath, without the loss of a rise or fall of a Wall Street fraction. The formal breakfast or lunch is more especially the feast of literary men, fashionable women, and other idlers. At their "receptions" our dames generally serve up chocolate and cakes. Tea, and *bouillon* in cups, which is simply beef broth, are also occasionally proffered to the most intimate friends. We are sorry to learn that the wine and *liqueur* decanters are beginning to circulate with unusual freedom at these gatherings of the gentler sex, though unprovoked to indulgence by the example of the grosser instincts of man.

There is much less formality in the serving of a lunch than a dinner. It is seldom in this country, though generally in France, composed of several courses. The whole repast, whatever it may be, is set before the guest at the same time. When one or two only are to partake of the meal, a tray is served; but when more, the whole table is spread, but every thing to be eaten ordinarily appears upon it.

The wedding, or formal official breakfast, is a stereotyped affair, cast in the moulds of the confectioner and restaurateur. It is little else than the fashionable ball supper, lighted up by day instead of gas light, and is composed, like it, of stewed oysters, galantines, mayonnaise of fowl, cold game, ices, pyramids, and all the knickknackeries of confectionery.

The proper costume at wedding and formal breakfasts, as at all festivals before dinner, is a morning dress. The gentlemen should wear frock-coats, and light vests and trowsers, and the dames their usual morning visiting drapery. The male visitor ordinarily enters the drawing-room with his hat in his hand, and the female will always, unless very intimate, present herself with her bonnet on her head. The guests take their places with all the ceremony of a formal banquet. The bride and bridegroom always have the precedence in the procession to the refreshment-room, and others take their position according to rank and age. The cavalier, in escorting his dame, should always give her his right arm.

The origin of dinner-eating is coeval with the creation of man. Dinner-giving, however, is the later product of advanced civilization. It may be received as an axiom that the social progress of a community is in direct proportion to the number of its dinner-parties. London, Paris, Vienna, Berlin, and other centres of refinement retain their pre-eminence by virtue solely of their daily banquets. Abolish these, and you extinguish the friendly relationship of nations, the intimate intercourse of the cultivated and refined, render "the feast of reason and the flow of soul" impossible, and arrest the progress of society. It is unquestionable that more enduring alliances have been struck by diplomatists across the mahogany than were ever agreed upon in ministerial cabinets. Talleyrand regarded the dinner-table the best place for the transaction of business; and while he himself was planted there, he could safely leave the rest to his subordinates and scribes in the office. The choice and costly dinners of Cambacèrès were ungrudgingly paid for by his master Napoleon, for he regarded and encouraged them as powerful engines of state. Who can doubt that much of the culture of the world, with all its elements of refined manners, intellectual converse, and taste for science, literature, and the arts, is largely dependent upon the social gatherings at the dinner-tables of the metropolitan cities? Trace the careers of any of the notable men of the world, and mark how often their genius is seen to sparkle at the convivial board. How much we should lose, for example, of Johnson, Garrick, Reynolds, Sheridan, Sydney Smith, or Theodore Hook, if deprived of their company at dinner! The general tone of science, literature, the fine arts, and taste, is unquestionably sustained by metropolitan social intercourse. If dinner-giving in its capitals were abolished, all Europe, we believe, would relapse into barbarism. In seeking for evidences of American progress in refinement, we should count the number of daily dinner-parties, on the great increase of which of late there is reason to congratulate not only all lovers of good cheer, but friends of their country.

The number of persons at a dinner-party, according to an old saying, should never be "more than the Muses [nine], or less than the Graces" [three]. Brillat Savarin says: "Let not the number of the company exceed twelve." He, like all his countrymen, stops suddenly short of the thirteen—an ominous number in the superstitious fancy of the French. Having the belief that this number will be sure to be fatal within the year to some one of the company, it is impossible to persuade thirteen to sit down together at dinner. The host, even, or some accommodating guest, whatever may be the occasion, will be sure to subtract himself from that odd and inauspicious sum, should it be unfortunately cast up at a convivial entertainment.*

It is too much the practice, particularly in this country, to invite people of the same profession or occupation to dine together. Apart from the fact that there is usually less harmony among such, and they are almost sure, like members of the same family, to quarrel with each other, there is this further objection, that their conversation is apt to be exclusively professional. If all divines, their talk will be divinity; if all lawyers, law; if all doctors, medicine; and if all merchants, trade. The result, of course, can not be

* It would seem from this record, taken from a French paper, but accredited to an English one, that the same superstition prevails in England: "Died, John Andrew Malkeith, aged fifty-four. His business was that of a *quatorzième*, or fourteenth man at table. He was thus often employed to dine three or four times on the same day, and had accumulated by the exercise of his functions, which were liberally paid, the sum of $100,000!"

very grateful to the dames who may be present, who will not care, probably, to be regaled in the intervals of the soup and fish, or the roast and dessert, with the perplexities of faith, the uncertainties of justice, and the nauseous details of physic. Brillat Savarin, than whom there is no better authority, says that the guests invited to a dinner "should be so selected that their *occupations shall be varied*, their tastes analogous, and with such points of contact that there shall be no necessity for the odious formality of presentations."

The invitations, if the party is a formal one, should be sent about a week or ten days before the dinner. The usual formula is simply this, either written in a note or printed on a card:

"Mr. and Mrs. ——— request the pleasure [or honor] of Mr. ———'s company to dinner at — o'clock on ———.

"R. S. V. P."

A formal acceptance should read thus:

"Mr. ——— accepts with pleasure Mrs. ———'s invitation to dinner at — o'clock on ———."

All written invitations should be answered immediately in writing, but especially invitations to dinner, and should be complied with at all hazards. If, by any mischance—as the death of a relative, or some other serious cause—the guest, after having once accepted an invitation, is unable to comply with it, he must be careful to send notice of the fact, with his regrets, at the earliest possible moment.

At all dinner-parties the ladies and gentlemen are expected to present themselves in full evening costume. Delicate hosts and hostesses, particularly when the occasion is not a very formal one, will take care to keep their own dresses in due subordination, lest they may possibly outshine too evidently some of their guests, and unnecessarily put them to the blush. Thus a fastidious host will not seldom keep to his frock-coat and black cravat, with a nice consideration for some invited person who may by chance have neglected to put on the swallow-tail and white choker *de rigueur*.

Punctuality is essential to the perfection of dining, as it is to the proper performance of every other social duty. A half hour's grace used to be allowed, and it was not "the thing" to arrive at the exact time appointed. Fashion, however, now sanctions what common sense has always inculcated, and men of society are expected, alike with men of business, to be exact in their engagements.

On reaching the house, the gentleman, if accompanied by a lady, gives her his arm on entering the drawing-room, and the first person addressed should be the hostess. Very fashionable people have a footman at the door to announce the names of the guests as they present themselves. If this is not done, the host or hostess may introduce their visitors to each other, taking care to make as little fuss as possible about it. When introductions are dispensed with, as they may be with propriety, the guests should have no hesitation in conversing freely with each other as mutual acquaintances.

When the dinner is announced, which should be done by the servant simply saying "The dinner is served," a procession is at once formed. The host gives his *right* arm to the female guest who has the precedence from age, rank, or strangeness, and leads her to a place at the dinner-table on his right, he being at the head or at one side. Next comes the most distinguished male guest with the hostess.* She seats herself at the other extremity, or at the opposite side of the table, with her cavalier on her right. The rest follow in couples, ranked generally according to age, and as they enter the dining-room are placed so that the host may be flanked on either side by a dame, and the hostess by a cavalier.

* In England the hostess often remains with her cavalier, the most important male person, until the last, and performs the duty of pairing the guests.

The rest of the guests are arranged in successive couples, so that each cavalier will be between two dames, and each dame between two cavaliers, provided the sexual proportions of the party allow of such an arrangement. It is usual to separate the husband from his wife, and temporarily sever other domestic relations. This does not seem flattering to the conjugal and family ties, but the practical effect is undoubtedly good.

CHAPTER XVI.

Etiquette of the Dinner (*continued*).—After Dinner.

If you value your health you will take a substantial meal, call it what you please, at an early hour in the day, say at noon, or thereabout. Plain people devour this repast, terming it dinner, while the fashionable eat it with no less eagerness, but under the appellation of *luncheon*, or, as the French say, *déjeûner à la fourchette.* It is unquestionably favorable to the vigor of the body to supply it with a large, perhaps the largest, portion of its essential nutriment between twelve and one o'clock. The appetite is almost universally strong at this time, and the corporeal energies being in their fullest strength, the function of digestion is more readily and effectively performed. We have no objection to a late meal—in fact, a sound stomach requires it; but it is dangerous, nay, fatal, to postpone the satisfaction of a hearty appetite until the close of the day. We all require the early solid repast, call it what you may—dinner, luncheon, or *déjeûner à la fourchette.* The later meal, if subordinate, is also beneficial, and it matters not whether you eat it as the humble supper or as the stately dinner.

The mistake which is made by many who take a late dinner is, that they make it serve the purpose of both dinner and supper. Instead of taking in the middle of the day, as they should, a good deliberate meal, of which meat ought to form the chief part, they put off the appetite with a dry biscuit, which appeases hunger, but fails to nourish the body. It is dangerous to abandon the early dinner without an equivalent in the form of the solid luncheon. All epicures agree, moreover, that, to appreciate a *recherché* dinner, it must not be eaten with the voracity of the man famished by a whole day's hunger, but approached with the cool deliberation of a person in the full command of all his faculties, dietetic and æsthetic. This he can not have unless he has subjected his appetite by a proper satisfaction of its requirements at the early and natural feeding-time of the day. "To appreciate your dinner, you must eat lunch," is an axiom in the science of gastronomy.

Considering the fashionable dinner as dietetically subordinate to the solid noonday repast, the hour of its occurrence becomes of comparatively little importance. In England people seldom sit down to it before seven or half past seven or eight o'clock. In France six is the usual hour; and the fashionable people of the United States seem generally inclined to follow the French in this, as in other things. If our advice and a substantial meal at noon be taken, we would recommend the ceremonious repast of the day never to be eaten earlier than half past five.

The ordinary mode of serving a dinner is the French one. The various dishes are placed upon the table just as they leave the hands of the cook, and, being carved by host and hostess, are distributed by the servants to the guests. For formal occasions, however, the Russian mode, or the *dîner à la Russe*, has become fashionable. The dishes, when this style is adopted, are not served until cut up, when they are handed in succession to each guest by the waiters. The table is adorned in the centre with flowers, and fruit fresh and sugared, various galantines of fowl and game, and ornamental confectionery. The plates of soup are generally put on the table before the guests are called in, and a bill of fare, as well as the name of each person, to indicate the seat he is to take, printed or written upon a card, is placed on the napkin.

Under each soup-plate there is one of the ordinary kind. On the right of this there are a napkin, a piece of bread, four glasses—the tumbler first, then the Madeira, then the claret, and finally the Champagne glass. Two large knives and forks are placed with the knives on the right and forks on the left of each guest; and when the dessert is to be eaten, a silver knife and fork and spoon are served upon the small plate, with the finger-bowl and doily. The guest, on receiving these, spreads his doily on his left, deposits the finger-bowl upon it, and noiselessly sets his knife on the right and his fork and spoon on the left.

The first duty of the entertainer is to see that his friends are well served. "The host who has compelled a guest to ask him for any thing is almost a dishonored man." He should anticipate the wants of all.

The old rule that "no one asks twice for soup" may now almost be said to be true in regard to all the dishes. Such is their number, and the systematic succession in which they are served, that few want "more," or care to ask for it, for fear of deranging the order of a well regulated dinner. The host and hostess, however, when carving, will not fail to invite each guest to a renewed attack, especially upon the substantial dishes before them; but an excessive entreaty to eat is not in good taste, and a refined guest never expects it. In the Russian dinner the servants make a second round with all the articles except the soup, but the opportunity thus offered for "a cut and come again" is seldom availed of.

The guest should commence eating as soon as helped, and not wait, as some people, with a strain at excessive politeness, do, until all are served, and thus produce an awkward pause of staring expectancy.

The ordinary French dinner consists of soup, fish, *hors d'œuvres*, such as olives, anchovy salads, radishes, etc., eaten during the early pauses of the dinner; *entreés*, or side-dishes, consisting of *patés*, *croquettes*, etc.; roast meats, vegetables, and sweet dishes, such as puddings, soufflets, and hot confections; and, lastly, a dessert of cheese, fruits, cakes, sweetmeats, and ices. The coffee follows. These various dishes are served and eaten in the order in which they are named. We in this country vary somewhat the French mode. We eat, for example, potatoes with fish, and all other vegetables with the dishes of meat. The salad is eaten just before the sweets, and often with the roast fowl or game. The Earl of Dudley, an English lord and fastidious diner, used to say, "A good soup, a small turbot" (a fish we haven't in America), "a neck of venison, ducklings with green peas, or chicken with asparagus, and an apricot tart, is a dinner fit for an emperor—when he can not get a better." A still simpler one ought to content the sovereign people of a republic. Say: soup, salmon and peas, a pair of boiled chickens, and a roast joint, with the various vegetables, followed by a good pudding or tart, and the usual knickknackeries of confectionery. If a brace of partridges, or a pair of canvas-back ducks, with the accompaniment of either a salad or currant jelly, should be added, and eaten just before the dessert, the banquet will be one which ought to satisfy the most exacting of guests in this democratic country.

It is seldom now that there is any removal of the table-cloth or disclosure of the mahogany. This is rendered unnecessary by a free use of large napkins, which are so placed as to protect the main covers where exposed, and be readily changed without fuss or derangement of the general order of the service. When the dinner has been eaten, the French—and decorous people every where should do likewise—all rise together, cavaliers and dames, and return to the drawing-room in the order they left it. Here the coffee and tea, together with liqueurs, are served; and after an hour or so, unless the evening is to be prolonged by the arrival of additional company, and a supplementary dance or other amusement, the guests disperse to their homes. A call of ceremony upon the late hostess—which can be made in person or by sending a card, some time during the succeeding week—is the becoming thing, though often neglected by the ignorant or indifferent.

We need not go so far back into the elements of breeding as some writers on etiquette have done, and remind our well-bred readers that it is not considered polite to pick one's teeth with a fork at the dinner-table, and that the water in the finger-glasses is not to be drunk, but to be used to wash the hands. The various observances of dinner ceremony are not so frivolous as they may appear. For example, it will be found that it is most convenient *not* to take soup twice, *not* to put the knife into the mouth, and *not* to allow the waiter to serve the guests on the right. Two plates of soup are too much fluid for any stomach at the beginning of a dinner; a knife is a cutting instrument, and may do mischief if introduced between the lips; and nothing can be more awkward, as you will find on trying, than the attempt to take any thing from a waiter on the wrong, or right-hand side.*

* The servants should always serve each one at table on his left. There is a story told of a negro servant of Wash-

At a large dinner-party it is better to confine your powers of entertainment to your immediate neighbors, and avoid bawling out to those opposite or at a considerable distance from you. Where the service is limited, you—if of the masculine gender—must attend constantly to the wants of the dames immediately under your wings. Avoid all gross heaping up of your plate. As a general rule, refuse to be served with more than one kind of meat and vegetable at a time. There are certain things which are

ington, who, not being able to distinguish between the right and left, was instructed to serve the guests on the side where he saw no buttons, which it was then customary to wear in a single row on the right breast of the coat. With this guide Pompey found it plain sailing until there came a guest freshly arrived from France with the new fashion of a double row of buttons. Pompey looked first at the one side and then at the other, and was for a moment terribly perplexed. He, however, soon came to the wise conclusion that the gentleman, having two sets of buttons, was entitled to be waited upon all around, and accordingly grasping the plate with two hands, thrust it over the guest's head with a grin of triumph.

Servants ordinarily wear white gloves, or have the thumb wrapped in the corner of a napkin while handing any thing. Some would-be exquisite guests sit down to dinner gloved, but this is an inconvenient practice which an intelligent refinement does not recognize. Where the service is complete, a guest should not give unnecessary trouble to his neighbors by calling upon them to exercise any part of the functions for the performance of which a proper number of efficient persons are especially provided.

supposed to be sufficiently harmonious for a combination—as, for example, ham and boiled chicken, rice or potatoes and tomatoes. There is one good rule which, if followed, will make you an acceptable guest every where: Be not obtrusive. Do every thing smoothly and quietly. Talk in a low tone of voice, and handle your knife and fork and plate without clatter, and eat without any audible gulping and smacking of the lips.

It was once an essential part of the dinner-table etiquette in England, and in America by inheritance, for the ladies to retire after the dessert and a first round of the wine decanters. The confessed purpose of the practice was to allow the *gentlemen* to indulge freely in strong drink and loose talk, unchecked in their grossness by the restraining influence of refined women. Polished France has given us a lesson of better manners, and the social dinner is now less often marked by this coarse reminder of the divergence of the brutal instincts of one sex from the delicate sentiments of the other. The more refined people in England and the United States now generally adopt the French practice of all rising together from the dinner-table. The effect of this simple change in etiquette has been very great and most beneficial. Drunkenness, once a fashion and almost esteemed a social virtue, is no longer admitted in respectable company, but has been forced to slink away to the bar-room and other haunts of vice.

When the dinner is over and the half of an hour or so has been passed in talk and trifling with the dessert, the hostess gives the signal by rising from the table, and all return to the drawing-room in the order they left. Here coffee and tea are provided, and it is good taste to have them served with as little formality as possible. The less exhibition of the flunkey force on the occasion the better. The tray having been placed by the servant on the table, the dame of the house pours out the beverages, whatever they may be, and invites her guests to partake of them. The gentlemen, of course, take care of the ladies before they take care of themselves, but all is done quite unceremoniously. It is seldom, in fact, that a person takes a seat, but all remain standing, or walk about the drawing-room, conversing or admiring the pictures, articles of *virtù*, and whatever else may invite notice. The visit to the drawing-room, being merely designed to graduate the farewell, and thus render the departure less abrupt, is naturally informal, for it is but a ceremony in an incipient state of dissolution. The stay after dinner, unless additional company has been invited, and there is a supplementary evening party, is seldom prolonged beyond half an hour, when leave is quietly taken.

CHAPTER XVII.

Ancient and Modern Hospitality.—Etiquette of the Evening Party and Ball.—The Effect of late Parties.—Manners and Morals.—Treatment of Servants.

Hospitality, as practiced by our ancestors, can hardly be said to exist any longer. The word, in fact, is nearly obsolete. The ceremonious displays of fashion have usurped the place of the social entertainments of friendship. No one hardly pretends nowadays that, in spreading a table or opening his drawing-rooms, he is actuated by an impulse of generosity or friendliness. He is merely complying, as he is ready to acknowledge, with the exactions of fashion, and takes no more credit to himself for the profuse bounty of his dinners and costly splendor of his balls than for the graceful cut of his coat or elegant turn of his boot. His feelings have, in fact, no more to do with the one than his taste has with the other. Both are devised by a set of trades-people, who have become, by some means or other not easy to determine, the ministers of that power, of which, though no one knows the origin, all are forced to acknowledge the authority.

Balls, evening parties, soirées, receptions, or whatever else they may be called, are entirely arranged and controlled by Fashion and her administrators. The hired master of ceremonies, the upholsterer, the florist, the pastry-cook and confectioner, are, in fact, the dispensers of modern *hospitality*, if we may be permitted the sacrilegious use of that sacred word in such a connection.

The ordinary evening parties or balls of our large cities are so much alike, that a dame whisked off, in the old mysterious way of the fairy-books, from one to the other, and set down within the arms of a fresh cavalier, would hardly be conscious of a change even in the pair of mustaches by which her cheek is titillated in the waltz.

Cards are generally issued from ten days to four weeks before the ball or dancing-party to the various persons on the fashionable list, supplied by a Brown or some other hired undertaker of public ceremonials. This is the usual form of invitation, engraved upon a card or written upon note-paper:

"Mrs. A. [or B.] requests the honor [or pleasure] of Mr. ——'s company on the evening of ——, at half past eight o'clock. R. S. V. P."

The hour is more frequently left unmentioned;

and, even when specified, the guest is not expected to be punctual. None but the most intimate friends think of going to a formal and fashionable party, where there is to be dancing, before half past nine or ten o'clock, and an invited person may enter with propriety at any hour, however late, during the night. Whether an answer is requested or not by the letters R. S. V. P. (*répondez, s'il vous plaît*—"answer, if you please"), it must be sent in a day or two, and written in the same formal style as the invitation, the acceptance of which may be thus expressed:

"Mr. T. accepts with pleasure the polite invitation of Mrs. A. for the evening of ———."

A refusal should be written as follows:

"Mr. T. regrets that he can not accept the polite invitation of Mrs. A. for the evening of ———."

When an invitation is accepted, it must be, if possible, faithfully complied with. It is not seldom that an invited person takes an uninvited friend to a ball or evening dancing-party, but he ought not to do so without first asking permission of the giver of it. As he is not likely to be refused, he must hold himself entirely responsible for the character and conduct of his companion, who, previous to and after the party, should send a card.

It is a good rule for those who are not able or

inclined to dance to refuse all invitations to balls and other parties where the guests are expected to do so. This is, of course, not to be regarded as obligatory where dancing is but a supplement of the general business, and card-playing, conversation, and other occupations are to form parts of the social labor of the evening.

On descending from the dressing-rooms, which should be always provided, the guest makes his way at once to the dame of the house, and, after a conventional phrase or two, yields his place to the next comer. When a gentleman is accompanied by his wife or any other lady, he should always wait for her before entering the drawing-room, and, giving her his right arm, escort her to the presence of the hostess. It is regarded as decorous to abandon her then to the tender mercy of the general politeness. "You must never dance with your wife except as a freak, when every body else in the quadrille does the same," says a cold-blooded, but, we presume, an unquestionable authority.

The polite hostess takes care to mark her conduct for the night by a total abnegation of self. Her toilette is carefully subdued, so that it may not surpass the average splendor, and her triumphs are sought in the brilliancy of the occasion, and not in the *eclat* of her own personality.

She is constantly seeking opportunities of display for her guests, that they may shine in the brightest and most favorable light while she is obscuring herself. She is pre-eminently the entertainer, and seeks her own enjoyment in that of others. She especially takes care to treat all her guests with a zealous and equal courtesy. She recognizes no distinctions of rank, birth, or wealth, and acknowledges no precedence beyond what society universally exacts. She waives for the occasion all favoritism, and rather neglects a friend than fail to show attention to a stranger. In these days she has little to do with the more material part of the entertainment. The arrangement of this mainly devolves upon the florist, the conductor of music, the restaurateur, and the hired master of ceremonies, but she carefully sees to the fulfillment by each of his special vocation. At supper, of which she is the last to partake, she watches closely the conduct of the servants, and is quietly but constantly urging them to their duty. The husband or the gentleman of the house has subordinately the same offices to perform and bearing to maintain as the hostess, but, while she is more exclusively occupied with the male, he is particularly devoted to the female guests.

Every gentleman should escort a lady to the

supper-room, and, after attending to her wants or tastes, never forget to return with her to the ball or drawing rooms, for nothing can be more impolite than to leave an "unprotected female" to shift for herself amid the tumult of a crowd of modern party-guzzlers. During the dance all should be exclusively devoted to their partners, and never allow themselves to keep up, by conversation or the telegraph of the eye and face, a communication with others.

Even those people who are familiar with all the formalities of fashionable society are often the worst offenders against the common decencies of life. It may be as well to remind such that it is by no means decorous to pass most of the night in the dressing-rooms smoking cigars, and so infecting their persons with the disagreeable odor that their presence becomes insufferable to every decent nose. It should also be borne in mind that decorum in the use of wine is not to be measured by the generosity of the host in supplying it. The consumption, however, of Champagne is not seldom in proportion to its abundance, and there are, in consequence, occasional scenes at our dancing-parties which bring the Fifth Avenue very close to Water Street. Among the vicious results of ill-regulated fashionable intercourse are observable a want of respectful reserve between our young people of both sexes, an interchange of slang phrases, audacious and dangerous flirtations, and a general defiance of the prudent restrictions of home.

The length to which the ordinary dancing-party or ball is prolonged is a serious evil. In our working community there are but few who, if they dance all night, can sleep all day, for most of the gay cavaliers of the evening are the busy drudges of the morning. Our youthful damsels, it is true, by the mistaken indulgence of their parents, can, if their excited nerves will let them, sleep away as many of the twenty-four hours as they please, but their partners can not, for they are wanted, for the most part, at the shop and counting-house. The mere loss of sleep, the recuperative influence of which is so necessary, must be a serious damage to the health of the young gallants who strive to comply with the requirements both of fashion and business. We would advise our friends to be always among the earliest to leave a fashionable party. There is, moreover, no rule of politeness which exacts a very prolonged stay.

A visit is expected on some day during the week after a ball or evening party. A card will, however, be generally accepted from the busy male as a substitute, though a personal appearance is exacted from the more leisurely dame.

"There is a great deal of human nature in the world," said Jacob Faithful, and it is to be presumed that servants have their fair share of it. Housekeepers, however, would seem unwilling to concede this; and we should judge from the manner in which many of them treat their domestics that they regarded them as of an organization entirely different from their own, with no portion of that abundant human nature of which Marryat's hero spoke.

Servants are ordinarily regarded by their employers as so many pieces of mechanism constructed to do a certain quantity of work of a particular kind, according to their especial functions, whether as cook, nurse, chamber-maid, or waiter. There are indispensable household results to be accomplished daily. The beef must be roasted and the potatoes boiled, the baby fed and dandled, the rooms swept and beds made, the hall-door opened and table served, and the Irish Bridgets and German Katerinas are the machines provided to execute these operations. Should they by chance show any tendency to rest from work or diverge from its object, the ever-watchful superintendent infers that the machinery is imperfect, and rejects it. If Bridget, for example, should by hazard fancy that she was human, and fall in love with some stray Patrick, and Katerina, under a similar delusion, become conscious of a patriotic sentiment, and steal away with Hermann to the Schützenfest or some other festive reminder of the fatherland, they would be sure to be condemned as worthless by many mistresses of the household.

It is astonishing how completely the human nature of the servant is ignored by her employer. The single pair of stairs which leads from the parlor to the kitchen would seem to separate, as it were, by an unfathomable abyss, the woman above from the woman below. The former has no sympathy for the feminine instincts of the latter; she will not, in fact, admit of their existence. The mistress, however conscious of her own feminine tendencies and inclined to indulge them, will not recognize or give any scope to such in her servant. The former may coquet, love, and marry, and will complacently regard herself as fulfilling her vocation; the latter is forbidden the companionship of her male friends, and is denounced as a trollop if she is caught passing a stolen word to the baker or butcher at the back door. In England a female servant is always asked, before she is employed, whether she has any "followers." By "followers" are meant suitors. If the poor creature confesses to this very natural result of a pretty face or some other female attraction, she is condemned at once. This cruel exaction of the servant-woman that she should neither love nor be loved is also not unfrequently made in this country, though differently expressed. "No visitors allowed" is the usual form of the harsh ordinance of our task-mistresses.

The want of a due recognition of the claims of the servant to human sympathy is shown, moreover, in the habitual reserve of their mistresses. There is not only that cold formality of relation which forbids any warmth of attachment, but a studied avoidance on the part of the employer of all knowledge of the intimate and personal interests of the employed. Hence there is complete ignorance and a consequent want of mutual confidence. Fidelity can only come from love, and love implies intimacy. Mistresses, in fact, are not sufficiently intimate with their servants. If they have real dignity and a personal superiority of their own, they need not fear any degradation from a closer contact with their subordinates, for the advantage of height will only become more apparent by the opportunity of comparison with lowness.

A closer sympathy of the employer with the employed is particularly important as regards the servant in relation to children. The education of the latter is greatly dependent upon the character of the domestic with whom the child must be necessarily in constant and close communion. By improving her servant, the mother will find that she is indirectly but surely elevating her offspring.

A more complete recognition of the human element of the servant will be found not only advantageous, but may soon become absolutely necessary. The servant has her future in America as well as others. We can not always calculate upon the present supply of the raw material of Germany and Ireland, which requires only to be kept in working order by an abundance of beef, potatoes, and wages. Employers will be forced, sooner or later, to seek for their servants exclusively among civilized people, and to compensate them not only by a fair day's pay for a fair day's work, but by a treatment which will recognize to its fullest extent their human dignity.

There is no surer sign of ill breeding and ill feeling than the rude treatment of dependents. The obligation of civility to servants should be inculcated especially upon the young American, who ought to learn at the earliest period that the accidental relation of advantage of position, which is ever alternating in a country free from prescriptive right, gives no title to a haughty demeanor and a domineering conduct. The recognition of the mutual obligation of master and man, and mistress and maid, is a certain sign of the true gentleman and lady, who will never exact from those temporarily placed in subjection to them the civility they are unwilling to bestow. The "thank you," "please," and other courteous expressions of a kindly consideration of the obligation of the employer to the employed, will be freely proffered by all who are fully conscious of their social duties and willing to acknowledge them. Policy, as well as good breeding, inculcates the necessity of gentle treatment and courteous behavior to servants, who will seldom fail to respond with a more zealous service and a readier obedience to exactions and commands rendered less harsh and domineering by a soft word and a subdued mastery.

CHAPTER XVIII.

Visiting Lists.—Report of the Proceedings of a Morning Visit.—Etiquette of Visits and Cards.—New-Year's Visits.—At Home, or not at Home?—P. P. C.

Every dame nowadays has what is called a visiting list. This is composed of a number of persons of her own sex who spend money, dress, and make calls very much as she herself does. No other sympathy than is indicated by these is required by mutual visitors of the fashionable sort. They need not be friends; it is not, in fact, necessary that they should be acquaintances, and we actually know of two dames who not long since met in the street and looked into each other's face as perfect strangers, though they had been on visiting terms for the last ten years or more. There is so little substance in this kind of social relationship that its obligations can be as well performed by a mere symbol as the person it represents, and thus a bit of card-board, with nothing but a name upon it, frequently serves every purpose.

Visitors, however, do occasionally meet, and, according to a very good authority, this is the result:

Mrs. A. "How delighted I am to see you! It is an age since I have had this pleasure! What a charming bonnet!"

Mrs. B. "You think so?"

Mrs. A. "It is perfect! But any thing upon you looks well."

Mrs. B. "I never saw you looking better; that morning dress is so becoming! I have just left Mrs. C. She was horribly dressed."

Mrs. A. "How can it be otherwise with such an ugly creature? What a beautiful sack that is! Who made it for you?"

Mrs. B. "Madame Bonnechose. Have you seen Mrs. C. lately?"

Mrs. A. "No; and I don't care to see her; she is such a fool. You know that affair?"

Mrs. B. "Yes; with Mr. T."

Mrs. A. "I will have to refuse to see her if she calls again. You are going already?"

Mrs. B. "Yes; I have some shopping to do."

Mrs. A. "Don't be so long again, my dear Mrs. B., before coming, and another time don't go away in such a hurry."

Soon after the departure of Mrs. B., who goes to another house, where she reports that Mrs. A. was looking as yellow as a pumpkin, and wore *such* a common-looking morning dress, Mrs. C. and Mrs. D. arrive.

Mrs. A. "How kind it is of you to call! It is an age since you have done me this favor! What a beautiful lace veil! my dear Mrs. C.; and those shoes of yours, Mrs. D., are exquisite; but no wonder, with such feet!"

Mrs. D. "Don't talk of my feet; it's you who have a foot worth talking about."

Mrs. A. "Mrs. B. has just been here."

Mrs. C. "Why, she told me she didn't visit you any more."

Mrs. A. "What! If she don't take care, what she says may come true. You know what people say about her—"

Mrs. D. "It's disgusting!"

Mrs. A. "She had the ugliest bonnet on you ever saw; and such a sack! I could hardly keep from laughing. And such a bore! I could hardly get rid of her. You are going already? Don't be so long another time before coming to see me; and try, when you do come, my dear Mrs. C., and you too, my dear Mrs. D., to stay a little longer."

If such, as it has been reported to us, is the result of these fashionable visits when made in person, then, for goodness' sake, let them be performed symbolically, and those fine dames of "society," Mrs. A., Mrs. B., Mrs. C., and Mrs. D., spared the necessity of opening their mouths and letting out vipers and toads, like the little girl in the fairy tale, and the other abominable things of scandal and falsehood.

There are certain occasions when society exacts the payment of formal visits, as, for example, in exchange for a call of courtesy; after an invitation to a dinner, ball, or other ceremonious entertainment; after weddings, births, and funerals; on any occasion deemed worthy of personal congratulation; on the return of a visiting acquaintance to his residence, whether in town or country; and on the arrival and stay of a visitor at the house of a friend.

It would seem to be the object of modern fashion to interpose as many formalities as possible between the members of society, in order to prevent intimacy of contact. This, perhaps, is a necessary result of the immense expansion of the great cities, and the consequent widening of the social relation. It would be manifestly impossible, if every fashionable acquaintance became an intimate friend, and thus entitled to the freedom of familiarity, to retain any of that personal reserve which is essential to self-respect. No one, moreover, with even the smallest visiting list, if each person in it had the liberty of an intimate, and could present himself when, where, and how he pleased, would be able to find time for the performance of the ordinary duties of daily life. It is well, perhaps, therefore, that a bit of card-board, with nothing but a name upon it, has been generally accepted as a symbol of, and substitute for the formal visit. All society has reason to rejoice in a device by which the bore has been politely but effectually balked of his victims. On most ceremonious occasions, therefore, the bit of pasteboard is gratefully accepted in lieu of a visit. There is no fixed regulation in regard to the size, form, and character of the card and the inscription, but all extremes and marked peculiarities should be avoided. It is customary to prefix to the name military and naval indications of rank, the ordinary titles of Mr., Mrs., and Miss, and the professional ones, such as Right Rev., Rev., and Dr.; but in this country Hon. and Excellency, for which there is no warrant but courtesy, are never taken by the unassuming. The address is generally engraved in modest letters in a corner. It is deemed proper for a person to leave the card himself, or send it by his own servant, but not by the post or street porter. When one calls with the view of making a personal visit, and is not admitted, he indicates the fact of its personality by turning down a corner or broad edge of the card. This, however, may be but a caprice of fashion, destined soon to yield to some other of a totally different kind. Even when admitted to a house it is right to give the servant a card, by which the person visited may be made unmistakably cognizant of the name of the visitor. If there are several persons in the same house entitled to calls, a card should be left for each. A male visitor ordinarily takes off his great-coat before entering the drawing-room, but carries his hat in his hand. His visit should be short, and generally brought to a close whenever another, who is not a common friend of himself and the mistress of the house, arrives.

In France, whenever a new-comer of recognized respectability fixes his residence in a place, he or she is expected to make the first calls. This, however, is not the rule in England and America, where the settled residents are expected to pay the initiatory courtesies, although in the large cities, when a family returns after a considerable absence, it is not unusual to send cards to their friends as an announcement of their arrival, and to make known their address.

New-year's calls are very much like other visits, except that they are made exclusively by the male sex, a wider range of time is allowed for them, say from ten o'clock in the morning to nine o'clock in the evening, and a greater display of toilette on the part of the ladies who receive is expected. The gentlemen present themselves ordinarily, as on other visits, in the fashionable costume of the morning and promenade, and not in the dress-coat and other parts of the dinner and ball array. The stay is commonly very short, and seldom continues after the arrival of a fresh-comer. A great latitude is allowed to the use of cards, and the introduction by a visitor of his friends and acquaintances. The refreshments may be more or less abundant and varied, according to the hospitable disposition and taste of the hostess. With the increase of the great cities, and the consequent enlargement of our social circles, there is a growing disposition on the part of fashionable dames to refuse themselves on New-year's Day to all but relatives and intimates of their families.

The politest receivers of a visit, if of the female sex, are not expected to do more than bow the head, say a gracious word or two of farewell, and ring the bell for the servant to open the street-door on the departure of a male guest. Women, however, are always treated with a more condescending courtesy by the well-bred even of their own sex, who will rise and accompany them at least as far as the drawing-room door, while a gallant man who has been honored by a visit from a lady will escort her to the last exit from his house, and even to the steps of the carriage, if there should be one awaiting her. Discreet visitors, ever mindful of the suggestive line—

"Welcome the coming, and haste the departing guest,"

will linger as little as possible *in transitu* from door to door.

We need not make use of the conventional lie, even if justified by the moral philosopher Paley, which asserts that we are "*not*," though we are "at home," when it is convenient, for any reason whatsoever, to refuse a visitor. The most fastidious sensibility should not be offended at the simple and honest word "Engaged," civilly softened by the tact of a judicious servant.

It is the general custom for those who profess to comply with the exactions of fashion to pay a farewell visit to their acquaintances when about to leave a residence forever or a considerable time. Cards, however, are ordinarily substituted for a personal interview, and upon these are written P. P. C. (*Pour prendre congé*), "To take leave."

CHAPTER XIX.

American Titles.—Proper Forms of Address.—The Use of the "Sir" and "Madam."—Professional Titles.—How to address Letters.—Esq.—Female Titles.—Nicknames.—Introductions.—Letters of Introduction.—Presentations to Court.—Visits to the President.

THERE is an evident tendency with us democratic Americans to supply our want of authorized social distinctions with titular appellatives, which have no warrant beyond the impudent assumption of those who take, or the flattering courtesy of those who give them. The titles which distinguish rank in the army and navy, and are of obvious use, are the only ones recognized by American law. The "Excellencies" and "Honorables," so profusely distributed among the numerous successful aspirants for popular favor, are, whether given to the august chief magistrate of the republic, or to the illiterate alderman's assistant of the lowest municipality, equally without sanction.

These unauthorized titles are used with the profusion with which they are bestowed. While, in most of those countries where social distinctions are recognized by law, it is considered good breeding to avoid in conversation the frequent repetition of the titles which mark them, in the United States the various denominations of fanciful rank are heard in every phrase.

The ordinary "Sir" and "Madam," to one of which we all consider ourselves more or less entitled, are uttered with a frequency and an emphasis which, though evidently intended to be courteous, would be regarded in England as impolite. We seem to have borrowed our manners in this respect from the French, who lose no opportunity of announcing the "Monsieur," "Madame," and "Mademoiselle." Our English relatives avoid the repetition of the "Sir," "Madam," and "Miss," except when they desire to express a certain degree of coldness or severity, and a sense of superiority or inferiority. Servants, they say, must always remember their "My lords" and "My ladies," their "Sirs" and "Madams," and their "Masters" and "Misses," and gentlemen as carefully forget them.

The professional title of "Doctor" of Medicine is never omitted, for the obvious reason of the advantage to him to whom it belongs, and others, of having it as widely known as possible. The "Doctors" of Divinity and Civil Laws, also, though the purpose may not be so easy to explain, are generally spoken of and to by their titles, which, however, should not be very frequently repeated in a conversation addressed to themselves. "Judge" has been greatly vulgarized by its indiscriminate use and application in America, though never heard in England, and any man of taste entitled to it would consider himself doubtless more honored by a breach of ceremony in this respect than by its observance. While in the performance of his functions, and during his tenure of office, it may be useful and appropriate that the judge should be called "judge," but when off the bench permanently there can be no motive for retaining a title which is apt to be bandied about with the contemptuous familiarity of a nickname. "Governor," "Mayor," "Chancellor," and other civil denominations, should likewise be restricted in use to the duration of office.

Though it may not be good breeding to repeat too frequently in conversation with people the titles which may distinguish them, it is deemed courteous to give them all they can claim on the back of letters addressed to them. The President of the United States, the governors of the various states, and the ministers to foreign countries of different grades, have generally the prefix of "His Excellency" to their names. For example, it is usual to write "His Excellency General U. S. Grant, President of the United States," or simply "His Excellency the President of the United States." "The Honorable" is given to the judges of the Supreme Court, the various members of the cabinet, of the Senate, of the House of Representatives, the chief officers of the state governments, executive, legislative, and judicial, the mayor, aldermen, and assistant aldermen of the most corrupt municipalities, to a lower descent than which we may be spared the necessity of tracing it. "The Right Reverend" is inscribed on every letter to a bishop, of whatever denomination he may be, and "The Reverend" in all addresses to the clergy. "The" is an essential part of these inscriptions of honor, and should never be omitted.

The collegiate or University distinction of Doctor is never properly written in full as an address, but is thus inscribed: "John Smith, Esq., *M.D.;*" "The Rev. Jabez Poundtext, *D.D.;*" "The Right Rev. Boniface Ignatius Episcopus, *S.T.D.;*" "Timothy Smart, Esq., *LL.D.*" It is no compliment to those who have gained the title of Doctor to give it indiscriminately to every horse-drencher and starved apothecary. The titles of A.B. and A.M. are never added to the superscription of an ordinary letter. "Parson" is a good English word, but it has been so vulgarized and made a term of contempt that no clergyman is disposed to answer to it. It can only be respectfully used nowadays thus associated: "Parson of the Parish."

Every male person in this country feels himself entitled to have the "Esq."* at the end of his name, and any one who pretends to exercise his discretion in the use of it must do so at his own peril. Your Irish Bridget of the kitchen never fails to confer upon her dear Patrick of the stable-yard the "Esq.," and, with a superflu-

* The following are considered, in England, to have a legal right to the title of Esquire:

"The sons of Peers, whether known in common conversation as Lords or Honorables.

"The eldest sons of Peer's sons, and their eldest sons in perpetual succession.

"All the sons of Baronets.

"The Esquires of the Knights of the Bath.

"Lords of manors, chiefs of clans, and other tenants of the Crown *in capite*, are Esquires by prescription.

"Esquires created to that rank by patent, and their eldest sons in perpetual succession.

"Esquires by office, such as Justices of the Peace while on the roll; Mayors of towns during mayoralty, and Sheriffs of counties (who retain the title for life).

"Members of the House of Commons.

"Barristers at Law.

"Bachelors of Divinity, Law, and Physic.

"All who, in commissions signed by the sovereign, are ever styled Esquire, retain that designation for life."

ous generosity of honor, gives him, in addition, the prefix of "Mr.," and will thus write down his name, if she can write at all, "*Mr.* Patrick O'Shaughnessy, *Esq.*"

There are some people who are so generous of rank that they give it not only to the husband, who may be doubtfully entitled to it, but to the wife, who certainly is not. Thus we may occasionally see the inscription "Mrs. Doctor," "Mrs. Right Rev.," "Mrs. Rev.," "Mrs. Honorable," etc. These are, of course, inadmissible in polite society, though they find some warrant in German usage, which divides the smallest honor of the man with the woman; and thus the wife of Herr Kenchenjunge Grosenfat, chief scullion of the first cook of the grand chamberlain of the first minister to the Grand Duke of Pumpernickel, becomes "Mrs. Kenchenjunge Grosenfat, chief scullion, etc." Those women who in these later days have made good their right to be useful in the world, and fairly won their diplomas of theology and medicine, can justly claim to be distinguished by the titles which belong to them. We must of course, therefore, write "Mrs. Dr. Blackwell," or "The Rev. Miss Stone."

It is not uncommon in this country, in addressing a married woman, to give her her Christian name, thus: "Mrs. *Mary* Smith." This is not the practice of the English, who always prefix the husband's Christian name, thus: "Mrs. John Smith." Where the married woman is married to the eldest male member of the family, or is the only one of the name, she receives merely the title of "Mrs. Smith," while each of the others is distinguished by her husband's name: "Mrs. *Peter* Smith," "Mrs. *Jonas* Smith," etc. Whenever the eldest dies, the wife of the eldest son or brother, or whoever may be next in the order of succession, succeeds to the honor of namelessness. The Christian name must be given to all but the eldest of the unmarried daughters. She is "Miss Brown," while the others are "Miss Jane Brown," "Miss Susan Brown," etc. When all are addressed or spoken of together, we say "The *Misses* Brown," and not "*Miss* Browns."

In very formal letters it is usual to write in the third person, and then the various titles, "His Excellency," "Mr.," "Mrs.," and "Miss," are used. In more familiar epistles it is proper to write "Your Excellency," "Right Rev. Sir," "Reverend Sir," or "Reverend and dear Sir," "My dear Madam," "My dear Sir," and "My dear Miss Smith," but never "My dear Miss" only. The "my dears" may be omitted where the intimacy does not seem to justify them, and, as a general rule, young unmarried women should be addressed in the third person. In the address at the beginning of a letter, and in the courteous expression at the end, it is better to adopt the conventional phrase of the day. It is, for example, safe to keep to the words "Respectfully yours," "Your obedient servant," "Yours truly," etc., and make no attempts to rival the humorous felicities of Charles Lamb's epistolary endings.

All such abbreviations in speaking of persons as "Doc," a "Gent," an "M. C.," a "Reverend," a "Reb.," "Mr. A.," "Mrs. B.," "Mr. G. Smith," and "Mrs. G. Smith," and nicknames like "Prex," "Dominie," "Prof.," and others, are inelegant, to say the least, and the usage of which people fastidious of manners and in language are careful to avoid. "Governor," "the Old Man," or "Old Gentleman," "*Paterfamilias*," "the Old Woman," or "Old Lady," applied to one's father and mother, are not only vulgar, but irreverent. Young people should carefully eschew them, and take care to give their proper titles not only to their parents, but to all other persons who are their superiors and elders. They must never speak of these as "Smith," "Brown," or "Jones," but give them the conventional prefixes of "Mr.," "Mrs.," and "Miss."

The English have always been great sticklers for formal introductions, and the story is told of one who, eying with his glass a drowning fellow-mortal, refused to extend to him a saving hand because he had never been introduced.

The Americans have followed to some, though not to this absurd extent, the example of their transatlantic relatives. We are by no means so reserved as they. Democratic friction has necessarily broken up and rubbed off a good deal of the original crustiness of our nature. Casual intercourse between strangers in America is much freer than in England. The American, perhaps, is as wanting as the Englishman is abounding in reserve. The proper medium is between familiarity and resistance. In traveling, English constraint is often fatal to the general ease and cheerfulness, while American freedom is not seldom subversive of personal comfort. In the close proximity of a railway carriage, two strangers can make themselves mutually agreeable without any sacrifice of personal dignity, and it is certainly their duty to do so. The concessions on such an occasion are, of course, to be regarded as temporary. They are drafts at sight on each other's courtesy, to be paid at date, and received as a final settlement which bars all ulterior claims.

The Americans generally are too indiscriminate in their introductions. They seldom allow two strangers to be together a moment without introducing them to each other. No presentations should be made without a regard to the mutual fitness and probable acceptability of the acquaintanceship about to be formed. No two should be introduced, however closely accident may have thrown them together, if they would be obviously incongruous as intimate associates. At a dinner or other party, all the guests are temporarily to regard themselves as acquaintances, and they require no farther introduction than the invitations they have received in common as the guests of the same host or hostess. Special presentations are quite unnecessary, and, when made, will indicate the desirableness of a permanent friendship.

In introductions, the introduced is presented to those who are entitled to precedence from sex, age, or rank. A gentleman, whoever he may be, is thus always taken to the lady, the citizen to the mayor, the mayor to the governor, and the governor to the president. In all cases but purely official or formal presentations, it is prudent, as well as polite, to secure the willingness of those whom you are about to commend to each other's intimacy.

Letters of introduction may be useful in a strange country as guarantees of social credit at home in the case of an emergency, when, for example, by some mishap or other, the more valid banker's one has failed. They have, however, lost much of their former power as a means of getting into foreign society. There is now so much traveling, and consequent abundance of these missives, that they have greatly diminished in specific value. If a stranger now gets in exchange for one of them a polite bow of the head and a vague offer of indefinite service, he must need be satisfied.

The ordinary letter of introduction is expressed in a few conventional phrases, as, for example:

"I have the pleasure of presenting to your acquaintance Mr. ——, whom I commend to your kind attentions."

It should be inclosed in an open envelope, on which, besides the address, it is customary to write, in the left and lower corner, the word "Introducing," followed by the name and title in full, clearly inscribed, of the bearer. When the letter is to be delivered, it should be sent to the person for whom it is intended, with a card on which are the name and address of the person introduced. The response should be in the form of a call and an invitation to dinner, but this latter part of the civility is not always complied with.

A good many people think that they are

obliged to give a letter of introduction to every presentable person who may demand it, and this has led to the depreciation of this kind of social currency. It is perfectly conformable with the laws of courtesy to refuse such a favor merely upon the ground of unwillingness to take the liberty of presenting any one to the person to whom the introduction is asked.

All presentations to foreign courts are made through the national representatives, and the information in regard to the various formalities required is obtained from them. The President's "levees" at Washington are open to the whole world, and are conducted with no more ceremony than an ordinary reception by any citizen's wife. The doors of the White House may be said to be never closed, and every one who pleases may call upon its occupant as upon that of any other dwelling. He must, however, not always expect a personal interview. This, to be secured, must be sought in the company of some dignitary or intimate of the President, who will thus be able to judge of the claims to attention of a visitor.

CHAPTER XX.

Births and Christenings.—Giving of Names.—Presents.—Visits.—Caudle Parties.—Etiquette and Ceremony of Marriages.—At Church.—In the House.—Death.—Funeral Ceremonies.—Finis.

It is Sir Thomas Browne, we believe, who, like Captain Shandy, deplores, and Voltaire, we know, who sneers at the fact that so noble a being as man has not a more glorious entrance into the world. Those who may be disposed to grow sad with the one, and smile scornfully with the other at the informal manner in which Nature presents us all to society, have no reason to question the ceremoniousness of the reception of those whom Fashion takes with its dainty hands, and acknowledges as its own.

No sooner has the doctor or nurse rejoiced the heart of the opulent Smith or Jones with the announcement that the chances of the extinction of the race of Smith or Jones are diminished by the birth of the "finest baby ever born," than haste is made to give the widest diffusion to the important fact. In England a birth of "respectability" is at once published in the London Times, and the news thus conveyed to the four quarters of the globe. In the United States, from an affected delicacy of reserve, we believe it is not usual to announce in a newspaper our periodical domestic issues. It, however, is the most convenient medium for spreading the intelligence of a fact which it is desirable to convey to all friends and acquaintances.

Soon after the news of a birth, however it may arrive, is received, female friends send their cards, and ask in regard to the health of the mother, who, when she is well enough, returns them "with thanks for kind inquiries." Personal visits are then expected, and these must be paid with the utmost punctiliousness. Male friends are not expected to call on such occasions, at any rate upon the mother. They may, however, visit the father, and bestow their congratulations upon him, as well as make the politest inquiries in regard to his wife and offspring.

The first great social event in which the newcomer is deeply interested, though not personally consulted, is the bestowal of the name by which he is thenceforward and forever to be recognized in the world.

Parents are apt to think that they have the right to call their children what they please. We would remind them, however, that, apart from the claims of good taste, which should never be disregarded, every mother's son and daughter have a vested interest in the names bestowed upon them. Parents have no right, socially, to disqualify their offspring by affixing to them either inappropriate or unseemly appellations.

There was more truth than oddity in Captain Shandy's notion that a great deal more depended upon the choice and imposition of Christian names than what superficial minds are capable of conceiving. "How many Cæsars and Pompeys, he would say, by mere inspiration of the names, have been rendered worthy of them! And how many, he would add, are there who might have done exceeding well in the world had not their characters and spirits been totally depressed and Nicodemus'd into nothing!" We commend this Shandean notion to every parent, who we hope, however, may escape the Shandean fate of having a Tristram in the family.

In well-regulated families the simple rule is followed of giving the children the names of their grandparents, parents, and other relatives. In Scotland the first son is named after the father's father, the first daughter after the mother's mother, the second son after the father, and the second daughter after the mother. This is a good general rule to follow, which, however, admits of exceptions. No one, for example, should perpetuate an ancestral name which has graced the Newgate Calendar, been affixed to the village stocks, or swung from the gallows-tree. If the appellation, moreover, should be positively ugly, it ought to have the go-by. There is nothing gained by reviving the Hezekiah Hogsflesh, for example, of some near relative, however reputable and dearly beloved. Parents can do no better than strengthen the family bond of union by a repetition to the farthest generation of the family names from which the ugly and disreputable have been weeded out.

The prevailing Christian names in an English or American family are an indication more or less of its origin. The predominance of Franks, Charleses, Hughs, Isabels, Louisas, Catharines, etc., is a proof of Cavalier, as that of Hezekiahs, Reubens, Jonahs, Jonathans, Rebeccas, Marthas, etc., is of Puritanic descent.

Names, however, are now frequently given which indicate nothing more than the peculiar sentiments, tastes, caprices, and fancies of those who bestow them. The pious are apt to turn to the Bible for a choice, and affix to their children, with a fond and almost superstitious hope of sanctification, the names of some patriarch, saint, or apostle. It is curious how little discrimination is sometimes used in selecting appellations from the Holy Book, which is supposed with simple reverence to render sacred every thing it may contain. We have all heard of the mother who insisted upon calling her first-born Beelzebub, for it was, she declared, a Scriptural name, which none could gainsay. We know two promising scions of a serious family who bear respectively the names of Abiathar Benajah and Jonah Jonathan.

The sentimental are apt to be guided by the last novel they have read, and to borrow the name of a favorite hero or heroine for the beloved son or daughter of their house. "Our second child, a girl," says the Vicar of Wakefield, "I intended to call after her aunt Grissel; but my wife, who during her pregnancy had been reading romances, insisted upon her being called Olivia." A respectable citizen of New York bears the name of "Orondates," borrowed by his mother from the hero of some forgotten novel.

The patriotic choose national names, and thus the Patricks abound in Ireland, the Georges in England, the Andrews in Scotland, the Hermanns in Germany, the Louises in France, and the Washingtons and Franklins in the United States. The scion whom we know, of an intensely loyal sire, bears the Christian name of George *Rex*. The following is the history given by General Grant's father of his son's name:

"It occurred in this way: he was our first-born, and his grandfather, grandmother, and several others felt an interest in naming him. We finally agreed to write all the names we chose (one each, there being seven of us), place them in a hat, and draw, abiding by the result. Ulysses was drawn *first.* But his grandfather's choice was Hiram. So, to please my father, we permitted it to be Ulysses Hiram; but all know how they got his name Ulysses S. on the West Point books. I tried to get it corrected, but Ulysses said he didn't like the name Hiram any way, and so we let it stand. We have never had any reason to object to it since."

In selecting the names of distinguished people for their children, it would be wise for parents to await the full verdict of posterity before committing themselves to any one's reputation for greatness. It is not safe to assume the excellence of any contemporary name, and affix to a child a supposed honorable appellation which time may turn into a stigma of disgrace. During the honorable period of Benedict Arnold's and Aaron Burr's careers, children were not seldom called after them, who grew up to a consciousness of the shame of bearing the names of traitors.

It is better, perhaps, to avoid altogether the names of mark, for the children who bear them will necessarily suffer by the continually suggested comparison with those who first bore them. If their careers should be humble, their humility will be increased; if aspiring, their utmost reach will be deemed a shortcoming. Ridicule or disappointment must be the inevitable result. No William Shakspeare Smith, Francis Bacon Jones, Isaac Newton Brown, Julius Cæsar Jenkins, or Marcus Tullius Cicero Higgins can ever, by any possibility, however gifted by nature and improved by art, reach a degree of poetry, philosophy, science, military heroism, or eloquence to justify his name, and, if but a simple mortal without extraordinary endowment, survive the ridicule of bearing it. An eminent author has committed this error in regard to his children, among whom there are a Sydney Smith, a Francis Jeffrey, and an Alfred Tennyson. He, however, thought, no doubt, that the splendor of his own name was such as to condemn already to comparative obscurity his offspring, and that they thus might not be harmed by any additional contrast of brilliancy reflected from his distinguished contemporaries.

If parents are, for want of family names, in search of others for their children, we would commend them to the familiar and unobjectionable, or "neutral" ones, as Sterne terms them, of William, John, Francis, Charles, Henry, Mary, Margaret, Louisa, Sarah, Helen, etc. The early English names are getting greatly into vogue; and you may hear in almost every nursery the pretty appellations of Arthur, Edith, Ethel, Edgar, Alfred, and Edwin. These are mellifluous, and come from ancestors common to Americans and English, by both of whom their memory deserves to be perpetuated.

The christening is most frequently, though not always, associated with the baptism, which is regulated according to the ecclesiastical formulary of the peculiar sect to which the parents of the child may belong. In the Episcopal Church there are always three sponsors or god-parents chosen from among the relatives or most intimate friends, and one of them should be he or she after whom the child is named. For a boy there must be two godfathers and one godmother, and for a girl two godmothers and one godfather. These, however they may neglect the religious responsibilities they assume, must never shirk the obligations which society imposes upon them of making a present to their god-children. This is ordinarily a silver mug, a knife, fork, and spoon of precious metal, some costly piece of laced costume fit for babyhood, or, if the piety of the giver should justify it, a handsomely bound Bible.

The convivial part of a christening consists of a luncheon or *déjeûner à la fourchette*, to which the relatives and most intimate friends are invited, and generally without the formality of a card or a note. On such an occasion it is usual for the chief male sponsor to propose the health of the infantile member of fashionable society in whose honor the meeting has been convened.

Some mothers, when ready, after the four or five weeks of seclusion exacted by a fastidious fashion, to face their female friends, find it convenient to assemble them together at a "caudle" party, when it is not essential that the refreshment should be confined to the ancestral spoonmeat from which the name is derived. The table is spread on such occasions with the usual constituents of the fashionable luncheon or breakfast, with the addition of cocoa, perhaps, or some other simple beverage, to give an innocent, convalescent look to the banquet.

Few, however Quakerish they may be in their opposition to ceremonials generally, resist, on marrying, the ordinary formalities of the wedding. We shall not pretend to give, as some have assumed to do, formularies for making love or plighting troth, but we doubt not that many a person has been left to pine away in single misery for want of knowledge of the proper procedure, simple as it may be.

It is customary in every country but our own, we believe, to ask the permission of the parents of the beloved one before formally proposing to her. The proposition being made and accepted, a ring, called "the engagement ring," usually containing a single diamond, of the highest value to which the generosity and means of the giver are capable of attaining, is presented by the successful suitor to his betrothed, who wears it ostentatiously on the ring-finger of her right hand.

The ceremony of marriage may take place as soon or long after the engagement as may be convenient to the parties most concerned. Until then, in our country, the intimacy of the betrothed is left unchecked by parental interference. The two are allowed to be and to appear every where together, and ordinarily show themselves in the public streets and promenades linked arm in arm.

When the day for the marriage is fixed, the future bride pays, in company with her mother, her last maiden visits. About ten days or a fortnight before the day of the ceremony, cards are issued. These consist of the separate cards of the bride and bridegroom, and two cards of invitation, on one of which there are merely the name and situation of the church, with the date and time of the ceremony, and on the other the names of the parents, thus associated: "Mr. and Mrs. John Smith," and an invitation to the house conveyed by the words "at home," with the address of the paternal mansion, and the date and hour of the reception. All these cards are put into one envelope, and sent to the relatives and intimate friends of both parties. The card conveying the invitation to the house is left out of those intended for mere formal acquaintances.

Presents are expected from the connections and friends, and the quantity and value of these have become of late so excessive, that the obligation to give them is felt by all but the richest and most prodigal to be very burdensome. They are often of a marvelous inappropriateness. We have known a silver tureen sent to a young couple whose prospects in life hardly indicated the probability of even a regular supply of the simple pot of soup which good Henry the Fourth of France wished to be the least daily portion of every one of his subjects. The presents, with the cards of the givers attached, are sent some days before the reception, that they may be displayed on the occasion. This public show of the donatives of the prodigal seems to have been ingeniously designed for the purpose of stimulating the lagging generosity of others, and thus keeping up a practice very grateful, no doubt, to each recipient, but exceedingly painful to most givers.

The ceremony of marriage is ordinarily governed by the ecclesiastical formularies of the sect to which the bride may belong, who chooses the clergyman for its performance. The bride has generally two bridesmaids, and the bridegroom the same number of groomsmen, but they may be both increased. The marriage is ordinarily performed at 12 o'clock in the day, at the church, which is first entered by the bride resting on the arm of her father, uncle, or whomsoever is to "give her away." Next comes the bridegroom, with the mother or nearest matronly female relative. Then follow the groomsmen and bridesmaids, arm in arm. The immediate relatives complete the procession to the altar, where the bride and bridegroom take their places in advance, with the parents a little behind, and the rest gathered in a group about them. The bridegroom takes care to provide the wedding ring, and have it in readiness at the proper moment when called upon to put it on. He then places it on the third finger from, but not counting the thumb of the left hand. When the ceremony is over, the question sometimes arises whether the bride is to be kissed by the bridegroom. We should leave its decision to the instinct of affection were we not solemnly warned by a portentous authority on deportment that "the practice is decidedly to be avoided; it is *never* followed by people in the best society. A bridegroom with any tact will take care that this is known to his wife, since any disappointment of expectations would be a breach of good breeding. The bride is congratulated by all her friends in the church, and elderly relatives will kiss her in congratulation." This is, of course, now settled beyond all peradventure of doubt by the fact that, according to the same authority, "The queen was kissed by the Duke of Sussex, but *not* by Prince Albert."

The married pair then return to the bride's house together, taking precedence of all, and, on arrival, assume a standing position at one end of the reception-room and await the coming of the invited guests, who, as they enter, are conducted by the groomsmen to offer their congratulations.

The conventional breakfast or lunch closes the ceremony.

The dress of the bridegroom is regulated by

that chosen by the bride; if she wears a white veil, he is expected to appear in black trowsers, dress coat, which may be either black or blue, white waistcoat, and white cravat; or, if a naval or military person, in full uniform. If the bride should prefer to wear a bonnet, the bridegroom should put on a frock-coat of black, brown, or other tasteful color, and light-colored waistcoat and trowsers. It is customary for the married pair to leave, on the day of marriage, for a tour, and remain absent for a week, ten days, or even more. On their return they expect visits from all those to whom bridal cards have been sent, and the usual succession of dinners and evening parties, after which they lose their distinctive character, and become incorporated into the vast mass of ordinary people.

The human body, even in the unconsciousness of death, continues to be the object of a punctilious observance of ceremony. The mourning relatives are usually spared many of the painful details of funereal civility by the convenient officiousness of the undertaker, upon whom devolve the chief arrangements of the burial and its attendant formalities.

We have shown the good taste in America of abolishing the hired mutes, the emblazonment of the emblematic horrors of death, the skull and cross-bones on the panels of the hearse, and all that "luxury of woe" so remarkable in the English funeral. We have borrowed from the French and the Germans the tasteful practice of the use of flowers. This, however, with our usual tendency to excess, has become immoderate, and there is often an ostentatious exhibition of a profusion of crowns, crosses, hearts, and stars of the rarest and most costly products of the hothouse, which seem rather an indication of the exultation of wealth than of a regret for the dead or sympathy with the living.

The notice of a death and invitation to the funeral are conveyed through the newspapers to the friends and acquaintances generally, but notes are sent to those who are to serve as pall-bearers. In this country ladies occasionally, but in England never, follow the procession, and the female members of the family not seldom make their appearance in company with the male chief mourners.

It is now beginning to be the custom in America, as in England, to send to relatives and friends cards edged deeply with black, upon which is printed or engraved the name of the deceased, with his age, place, and date of his death. These are acknowledged by letters of condolence sent immediately, and visits of ceremony after a proper time. With a singular preference of devotion to fashion, ladies, whatever may be the control of their emotions and disposition to perform their religious duties, abstain from going to church before, and for several days after the funeral. The card, and the letter-paper and envelope edged with black, are used during the whole period of mourning.*

* Mourning should be worn, as we are told by a professed authority,

"For a husband or wife, from one to two years, though some widows retain their mourning for life.

"For a parent or grandparent, from six months to a year.

"For children above ten years of age, from six months to a year; for those below that age, from three to six months; and for an infant, six or seven weeks.

"For brothers and sisters, six to eight months.

"For uncles and aunts, three to six months.

"For cousins, or uncles or aunts related by marriage, from six weeks to three months.

"For more distant relatives or friends, from three weeks to as many months, according to the degree of intimacy."

The servants are ordinarily put in mourning by those who can afford it on the death of an important member of the family. The nurse only in the case of the death of young children.

INDEX.

THE END.

USEFUL BOOKS FOR FAMILY READING

PUBLISHED BY

HARPER & BROTHERS, NEW YORK.

☞ *Either of the following books will be sent by mail, postage prepaid, to any part of the United States, on receipt of price.*

HARPER'S NEW MONTHLY MAGAZINE. 39 vols., 8vo, Cloth, $3 00 each; Half Calf, $5 25.

"The Best Monthly Periodical, not in this country alone, but in the English language."—*The Press*, Philadelphia.

HARPER'S WEEKLY. 13 vols., Cloth, $7 00 each; Half Morocco, $10 50.

"A complete Pictorial History of the Times."

HARPER'S BAZAR. A Repository of Fashion, Pleasure, and Instruction. 2 vols., Cloth Gilt, $7 00 each; Half Morocco, $10 50.

"The young lady who buys a single number of HARPER'S BAZAR is made a subscriber for life."—*N. Y. Evening Post.*

ABBOTT'S YOUNG CHRISTIAN SERIES. The Young Christian Series. By JACOB ABBOTT. Very greatly improved and enlarged. With numerous Engravings. Complete in 4 vols., 12mo, Cloth, $1 75 each.

THE YOUNG CHRISTIAN.
THE CORNER STONE.
THE WAY TO DO GOOD.
HOARYHEAD AND M'DONNER.

ABBOTT'S CHILD AT HOME. The Child at Home; or, the Principles of Filial Duty familiarly Illustrated. By JOHN S. C. ABBOTT. Woodcuts. 16mo, Cloth, $1 00.

ABBOTT'S MOTHER AT HOME. The Mother at Home; or, the Principles of Maternal Duty familiarly Illustrated. By JOHN S. C. ABBOTT. Engravings. 16mo, Cloth, $1 00.

BEECHER'S DOMESTIC RECEIPT-BOOK. Designed as a Supplement to her Treatise on Domestic Economy. By CATHARINE E. BEECHER. 12mo, Cloth, $1 50.

BEECHER'S DOMESTIC ECONOMY. A Treatise on Domestic Economy, for the use of Young Ladies at Home and in School. By CATHARINE E. BEECHER. 12mo, Cloth, $1 50.

THE TRAINING OF CHILDREN. The Religious Training of Children in the Family, the School, and the Church. By CATHARINE E. BEECHER. 12mo, Cloth, $1 75.

BURTON'S CULTURE OF THE OBSERVING FACULTIES. The Culture of the Observing Faculties in the Family and the School; or, Things about Home, and how to make them Instructive to the Young. By WARREN BURTON, Author of "The District School as it Was," "Helps to Education," &c. 16mo, Cloth, 75 cents.

BEMENT'S AMERICAN POULTERER'S COMPANION. A Practical Treatise on the Breeding, Rearing, Fattening, and general Management of the various Species of Domestic Poultry. By C. N. BEMENT. Illustrated with Portraits of Fowls, mostly taken from Life; Poultry-Houses, Coops, Nests, Feeding-Houses, &c., &c. With 120 Illustrations. 12mo, Cloth, $2 00.

COMBE'S TREATISE ON INFANCY. A Treatise on the Physiological and Moral Management of Infancy. For the Use of Parents. By ANDREW COMBE. From the Fourth Edinburgh Edition. 18mo, Cloth, 75 cents.

COMBE'S TREATISE ON DIGESTION. The Physiology of Digestion considered with Relation to the Principles of Dietetics. By ANDREW COMBE. Illustrated. 18mo, Cloth, 75 cents.

COMBE'S PHYSIOLOGY. The Principles of Physiology applied to the Preservation of Health, and the Improvement of Physical and Mental Education. By ANDREW COMBE. With Questions. Engravings. 18mo, Cloth, 75 cents.

DALTON'S PHYSIOLOGY. A Treatise on Physiology and Hygiene; for Schools, Families, and Colleges. By J. C. DALTON, M.D., Professor of Physiology in the College of Physicians and Surgeons, N. Y. With Illustrations. 12mo, Cloth or Half Leather, $1 50.

HOOKER'S CHILD'S BOOK OF NATURE. The Child's Book of Nature, for the Use of Families and Schools; intended to aid Mothers and Teachers in Training Children in the Observation of Nature. In Three Parts. Part I. Plants; Part II. Animals; Part III. Air, Water, Heat, Light, &c. By WORTHINGTON HOOKER, M.D. Engravings. The Three Parts complete in One Volume, Small 4to, Cloth, $2 00; or, separately, 90 cents each.

MACE'S PHYSIOLOGY FOR THE YOUNG. The History of a Mouthful of Bread, and its Effect on the Organization of Men and Animals. By JEAN MACÉ. Translated from the Eighth French Edition by Mrs. ALFRED GATTY. 12mo, Cloth, $1 75.

MACE'S PHYSIOLOGY FOR THE YOUNG. The Servants of the Stomach. By JEAN MACÉ, Author of "The History of a Mouthful of Bread," "Home Fairy Tales," &c. Reprinted from the London Edition, Revised and Corrected. 12mo, Cloth, $1 75.

OSGOOD'S AMERICAN LEAVES. American Leaves: Familiar Notes of Thought and Life. By Rev. SAMUEL OSGOOD, D.D. 12mo, Cloth, $1 75.

SMILES'S SELF-HELP. Self-Help; with Illustrations of Character, Conduct, and Perseverance. By SAMUEL SMILES, Author of "The Life of the Stephensons," "The Huguenots," &c. New Edition, Revised and Rewritten. 12mo, Cloth, $1 00.

THE STUDENT'S OLD TESTAMENT HISTORY. The Old Testament History. From the Creation to the Return of the Jews from Captivity. Edited by WILLIAM SMITH, LL.D. With Maps and Woodcuts. Large 12mo, Cloth, $2 00.

THE STUDENT'S NEW TESTAMENT HISTORY. The New Testament History. With an Introduction, connecting the History of the Old and New Testaments. Edited by WILLIAM SMITH, LL.D. With Maps and Woodcuts. 12mo, Cloth, $2 00.

STUDENT'S QUEENS OF ENGLAND. Lives of the Queens of England. From the Norman Conquest. By AGNES STRICKLAND. Abridged by the Author. Revised and Edited by CAROLINE G. PARKER. 12mo, Cloth, $2 00.

THE STUDENT'S FRANCE. A History of France from the Earliest Times to the Establishment of the Second Empire in 1852. Illustrated by Engravings on Wood. Large 12mo, Cloth, $2 00.

THE STUDENT'S HUME. A History of England from the Earliest Times to the Revolution in 1688. By DAVID HUME. Abridged. Incorporating the Corrections and Researches of recent Historians, and continued down to the year 1851. Illustrated by Engravings on Wood. Large 12mo, Cloth, $2 00.

A SMALLER HISTORY OF ENGLAND, from the Earliest Times to the Year 1862. Edited by WILLIAM SMITH, LL.D. Engravings. 16mo, Cloth, $1 00.

THE STUDENT'S GREECE. A History of Greece from the Earliest Times to the Roman Conquest, with Supplementary Chapters on the History of Literature and Art. By WILLIAM SMITH, LL.D. Revised, with an Appendix, by Prof. GEORGE W. GREENE, A.M. Engravings. Large 12mo, Cloth, $2 00.

A SMALLER HISTORY OF GREECE. The above Work abridged for Younger Students and Common Schools. Engravings. 16mo, Cloth, $1 00.

THE STUDENT'S ROME. A History of Rome from the Earliest Times to the Establishment of the Empire. With Chapters on the History of Literature and Art. By HENRY G. LIDDELL, D.D., Oxford. Engravings. Large 12mo, Cloth, $2 00.

A SMALLER HISTORY OF ROME, from the Earliest Times to the Establishment of the Empire. By WILLIAM SMITH, LL.D. With a Continuation to the Fall of the Western Empire in the Year 476. By EUGENE LAWRENCE, A.M. Engravings. 16mo, Cloth, $1 00.

TRACY'S MOTHER AND HER OFFSPRING. The Mother and her Offspring. By STEPHEN TRACY, M.D., formerly Missionary Physician of the A.B.C.F.M. to China. 12mo, Cloth, $1 50.

THE STUDENT'S GIBBON. The History of the Decline and Fall of the Roman Empire. By EDWARD GIBBON. Abridged. Incorporating the Researches of recent Commentators. By WILLIAM SMITH, LL.D. Engravings. Large 12mo, Cloth, $2 00.

VAUX'S ARCHITECTURE. Villas and Cottages: a Series of Designs prepared for Execution in the United States. By CALVERT VAUX, Architect (late DOWNING & VAUX). New Edition, revised and enlarged. Illustrated by nearly 500 Engravings. 8vo, Cloth, $3 00.

WATSON'S AMERICAN HOME GARDEN: being Principles and Rules for the Culture of Vegetables, Fruits, Flowers, and Shrubbery. To which are added brief Notes on Farm Crops, with a Table of their Average Product and Chemical Constituents. By ALEXANDER WATSON. With several Hundred Illustrations. 12mo, Cloth, $2 00.

WEBSTER'S DOMESTIC ECONOMY. Encyclopædia of Domestic Economy: comprising such Subjects as are most immediately connected with Housekeeping; as, the Construction of Domestic Edifices; Articles of Furniture; Animal and Vegetable Substances used as Food, and the Methods of Preserving and Preparing them by Cooking; Making Bread; Materials employed in Dress and the Toilet; Business of the Laundry; Preservation of Health; Domestic Medicine, &c. By THOMAS WEBSTER. With Additions by an American Physician. With nearly 1000 Engravings. 8vo, Sheep, $5 00.

WOOD'S PHYSICAL EXERCISES. Manual of Physical Exercises. By WILLIAM WOOD. Copiously Illustrated. 12mo, Cloth, $1 50.

WILLSON'S SCHOOL AND FAMILY READERS. A Series of School and Family Readers, aiming at the Highest Degree of Usefulness, and splendidly Illustrated. Consisting of a Primer, Two Spellers, and Seven Readers. By MARCIUS WILLSON. The Primer, Primary and Larger Spellers, and the First, Second, Third, Fourth, and Fifth Readers are now ready; also the Third and Fourth Intermediate Readers.

PRIMARY SPELLER	18mo	20
LARGER SPELLER	12mo	40
PRIMER. Engravings	12mo	25
FIRST READER. Engravings . . .	12mo	40
SECOND READER. " . . .	12mo	60
THIRD READER. " . . .	12mo	90
FOURTH READER. " . . .	12mo	$1 35
FIFTH READER. " . . .	12mo	1 80
MANUAL OF OBJECT TEACHING	12mo	1 50
INTERMEDIATE THIRD READER	12mo	80
" FOURTH READER	12mo	1 10

CALKINS'S NEW OBJECT LESSONS. Primary Object Lessons, for Training the Senses and Developing the Faculties of Children. A Manual of Elementary Instruction for Parents and Teachers. By N. A. CALKINS. Illustrations. 12mo, Cloth, $1 50.

www.ingramcontent.com/pod-product-compliance
Lightning Source LLC
LaVergne TN
LVHW010221110826
845151LV00004B/1164